Shopportunity!

Shopportunity!

How to Be a Retail Revolutionary

Kate Newlin

Collins

An Imprint of HarperCollins*Publishers*

HarperCollins books may be purchased for educational,
business, or sales promotional use. For information,
please write to: Special Markets Department, HarperCollins Publishers,
10 East 53rd Street, New York, NY 10022.

Designed by Jaime Putorti

Library of Congress Cataloging-in-Publication Data has been applied for.

ISBN-10: 0-06-088840-7
ISBN-13: 978-0-06-088840-4

06   07   08   09   10   DIX\RRD   10   9   8   7   6   5   4   3   2   1

*For Colonel Dale A. Newlin Sr. (deceased)
and his dear granddaughter, Mattie*

Contents

Introduction

What Becomes an Abandoned Superstore Most?

Visualize a long, wide, flat stretch of pavement. At its center is a triangular wedge of dirt, encased in concrete. This is a tiny Eden, perhaps seven feet at its widest point, but it is nonetheless a carefully landscaped and tended garden. Picture blue spruce and dusty millers, yellow daylilies and creeping juniper. See the hemlock too. We are in a deserted parking lot. Perhaps three cars huddle here, near Troy-Schenectady Road, only a mile or so from the larger and conspicuously full lot shared by Wal*Mart and Home Depot, even nearer the New York Route 87 exit ramp.

But this apparently abandoned site is not a lackluster entrant in a quest for price-sensitive shoppers. What was once a Grand Union grocery store and strip mall near the Albany suburb of

Latham, New York, has been reincarnated as Grace Fellowship Church. Its parking lot is empty for a reason. Today is Tuesday. Sunday, agitated drivers will jockey here for pride of place, too.

The low-slung building is fronted with the glass add-on structures more usually affixed to garden center stores. The entrance doors no longer open automatically, the gum-ball machines, grocery carts, coin-operated mechanical horse rides and neighborly bulletin boards are banished. No sign reminds us that ground chuck once sold here for $2.19 a pound, but we sense it. The air-conditioning offers that cherished jolt against the overwhelming humidity of a June day in a landlocked county. We are in a familiar setting, almost.

Once inside, it begins to get stranger quickly. The gray-blue carpeted entrance and, for now, desolate welcome area obliterate any vestige of a row of footsore cashiers under its italicized and chipper Information Center sign and plum-accented counter.

The silence disturbs. We miss the noises, the movements, the rat-ta-tat-tat of human commerce, of scanning products along a conveyor belt, of calling for price checks and check approvals, of making change and small talk. The mundane needs and momentary lusts of harried mothers juggling toddlers and coupons have retreated far from these barren aisles. Where there was once an Express Lane, there is now a tiny counseling office with two wing chairs and an artificial fireplace. But still, we can nearly hear the echoes of the old ADD-afflicted prayer, "Please, Lord, get me out of here."

We stand in the once-upon-a-time home to iceberg lettuce, snap peas, Chilean sea bass, ground chuck, frozen chicken nuggets, Kraft Macaroni and Cheese, Tide, Oreo, organic rutabaga, Pepsi, Heinz Tomato Ketchup and other nuts and bolts of modern life.

Twenty Delatour Road is a Grand Union of a different stripe. Forsaken by the grocery store chain attempting to crawl out from under bankruptcy, this Big Box now retails in spiritual wares. The photo array of pastor and elders succeeds an earlier showcase for the store manager and employee of the week. The sanctuary's mauve-upholstered, stackable chairs offer seating to 1,025; it has been architecturally primed to grow to 1,400 at any moment. Its Christian rock band–ready stage is complete with sophisticated audio calibrated from a production booth at the rear of the room. The 50-inch closed circuit TV screens stand mute and as ready to spring to life as the deep plush of the theatrical red velvet curtain is ready to part, to reveal, to enrapture.

We are in a familiar if not easily decipherable setting. Anchored by the knowledge that it is okay to choose among a set of equivalent brands, we are drawn calmly into the canon of mass-produced religion. It is all here for everyone—and it is just for you, your preferences, your predilections, your products, your way. In this case, regardless of whether you grew up Episcopalian, Lutheran, Methodist, or any other of 400-some flavors of Christianity, you are welcomed to a nondenominational brand of worship that opens its arms generally to all—and particularly to you. The serene environment is at once as universal and as specific as a grocery list.

"The fruits and nuts were over there," says Gerry Pettograsso, with the comfort of a canned witticism, as we look around the sanctuary and he points merrily to the far wall. He's the crew-cut, stocky, polo-shirted and chino-clad 50-something facilities manager and a church member.

The strip mall adjacent to the Grand Union has been annexed by Grace Fellowship as well. Now the reclaimed storefronts hold the nursery with its Disneyesque murals depicting Noah and the ark and Daniel in the lion's den in the bright primary colors designed to evoke the supersized glee more typically gleaned from Saturday-morning cartoons. (There is also a fresco depicting a hitherto unknown Bible story involving space travel and an astronaut.) Farther down the one-time shopping arcade passageway, Alcoholics Anonymous and other small-group meeting areas are revealed, along with adult classrooms and a work-in-progress library.

"We've been here three years," Pettograsso says, walking along the passageway. "A lot of the demolition was done by parishioners and most of the Sunday-school décor is volunteer work. Like the King Jesus Room," he says, opening one of a dozen doors.

The nameplate on the door ratifies his statement: This is indeed the King Jesus Room, decorated in a dark-gray palette and featuring a medieval theme, enhanced by a suit of armor and mock-up of a castle surrounding a small stage with microphones and sound equipment. It too is vacant; its use indecipherable. He moves along, toward the old warehouse: "The loading dock area is now the choir room."

Soon enough Pettograsso arrives at the site of another conversion: What was once the Home Style Buffet is now the home of the Grace Fellowship Youth Ministry, complete with DVD players, video games, walk-in refrigerators and live feed from the main sanctuary for services that overflow. Scores of television sets are placed strategically throughout the room, firmly attached, high on pillars. In the snack area, round black tables, each encircled by three black chairs, mimic the fluorescent-lit, potential intimacy of any fast-food franchise on any metropolitan thoroughfare, just before opening time.

Tomorrow night, this eerie quiet will be displaced by the din of teenagers convening with their parents' blessings to hang out. They'll trod the well-worn brown-and-black-patterned carpeting that rumples at the corners where it meets a wall. They'll slouch on the cast-off sofas scattered about the place. They'll give the old snow-cone machine another whirl, while considering the hereafter amid the here-and-now of high school gravitas.

The artist Julia Christensen, who has made it her project to study abandoned Big Box stores, explained it to me. "It's about the cars. These stores were built near access roads; that's the core idea. Before the advent of the automobile, everything was built within walking distance: church, stores, meeting places. The organizing principle was proximity.

"These Big Box stores exert the power they do and can be reconfigured for many, many purposes not because of the store, but because of the infrastructure that supports it: the roads, the parking, the accessibility within the sprawl of modern life, when driving 60 miles is no big deal."

Thus the megastore has become the megachurch. You don't need to be clairvoyant to intuit that, in a culture in which people speak of "shopping for a church," this makes a weird kind of sense. The sanctuary's ten-foot ceiling and fire-retardant, sound-enhancing acoustical panels do not force the worshipper's gaze upward. Natural light is nonexistent; no need for stained glass here. The weekday cool and calm is dizzying.

It is not that the buzz and moan of the marketplace—the clamor of people in search of new, better, faster, more, cheaper—has been stilled. It seems simply to sleep, ready to be roused. The form has, indeed, followed its function. We are still where we once sought whiter whites, brighter colors, and an end to ring-around-the-collar, but we search now for restoration of a more permanent kind. Nothing short of eternal transformation will do. An Oreo lasts only so long. The cereal gets soggy. The shirts become dirty again.

"The highlight of this assignment was the way that Grace Fellowship could quickly get into this place, compared to the long and expensive process of building new," says Todd R. Phillippi, president of Whitehead, Phillippi & Harris Inc., the architectural firm responsible for this conversion and several others around the country. Highlight? In a religion that once worshipped in cathedrals which took generations, even centuries to complete, cheap speed trumps painstaking workmanship.

"It also created a much friendlier environment for the unchurched," Phillippi explains. "People who might feel uncomfortable in the typical church-building setting."

How did this happen? We are more comfortable in a deserted Big Box grocery store than in a conventional church? How have we come to be comfortable in such an uncomfortable setting?

Grace Fellowship Church is simply one of dozens of deserted mega stores dotting the American landscape today. These massive constructions are being "repurposed" into a new shopping order—whether church, fitness center or local government service park. All the while the Big Boxes themselves lumber on, becoming ever bigger, ever meaner and more hostile environments, their wares becoming ever cheaper, their shoppers ever fatter, ever deeper in debt.

And, of course, not every Big Box is successfully "repurposed." According to one study, there are just about 27 million square feet of empty Wal*Marts dotting the countryside. It moves on, but leaves these vacant eyesores as testament to the path it is cutting through communities and our psyches.

The Big Box obsession with massive quantities of cheap goods has seeped into us. It has gone well beyond the products manufactured in the sweatshops of third-world countries. This zeal for getting "lots for less" sucks meaning from every aspect of our lives, debasing our religions, ethics, values, aspirations, tastes, families—our very selves. Meanwhile, what we really need is transformation in the opposite direction—toward more meaning, not less.

The products we seek can help us assert our significance, they can help us make sense of and find meaning in our lives, but the retail world in which we currently shop is seemingly hell-bent on thwarting us. This book is written to confront the troubling issues of our daily marketplace. We must ask: How has the *charming significance of things* lost out to low price? We must wonder if we've become *addicted* to the dopamine rush of getting a good deal and, like all real junkies, begun to confuse our wants with our needs. We must worry that we've lost awareness of our physical needs: No longer realizing we're no longer hungry, we subdue our instincts and better judgment and mindlessly gobble more than our bodies can bear. We must confront the psychic toll of pursuing a runway model's lifestyle with forged Chanel bags. We must acknowledge the cost of this tyranny of the cheap.

It is not enough to know the problems. We must plot a pathway out: We need practical ways, even rules, to revolutionize our retail experience. The best products, the best brands promise and deliver significant transformations: of our moods, of our roles in society, of our culture itself. So do the best retail experiences, lifting us aloft into a new world, into a new way of looking at this world. I want to look at the best and the worst shopping experiences today to understand both shopping's enduring allure—and the lost opportunity in the shop.

I want to understand why we're willing to pay $3.50 for a latte at Starbucks, but bristle at a 10-cent increase in the price of toothpaste. I want to learn why we'll drive miles out of our way to buy a bag of 100 razor blades for 50-cents less than at our local store, and then spend $3.99 on a tub of pretzels we didn't know we needed and that we'll resent having eaten once it's gone. I want to explore why a bookseller would offer me a steep discount on a book I'm ready to buy at full price and what this means to his ability to pay his staff—and to my evaluation of the book. I want to understand why we're shocked and outraged to pay $3 a gallon at the pump for gas, but eager to pay $1.50 for eight ounces of Poland Spring water inside the adjacent convenience store.

I want to identify serious options that work for all of us, consumers, manufacturers and retailers. We will map the frontiers of the marketplace, the edges of the known world of retailing where quality, joy, exuberance and valuable experiences persist. Indeed, I want to create the playbook, the new rules of engagement, marking the boundaries of what you're owed in a real *Shopportunity!* and what you owe—the part you play in restoring the thrill to the hunt. I search for ways to unearth the treasure currently buried in today's shopping experience.

This, then, is a journey we embark upon together, looking behind the scenes and bearing witness to the fact that one generation of marketers has addicted three generations to the heroin of everyday low prices. We will move onward to a reinvigorated shopping experience: The world of *Shopportunity!*—where the opportunity *is* in the shop.

I write this book as a business consultant who has witnessed this spiraling rush to the bottom from inside the corporate conference rooms of the Fortune 100. I've logged hundreds of hours watching and listening to consumers as they articulate their unmet needs, their unarticulated desires, their dashed hopes in the real world of retailing.

This is at once an insider's guide to the unrelenting, unrewarding and rabidly atrophying heart of cheapness in the world of consumer products and a passionate *cri de coeur* from an inveterate shopper who remembers and longs for the return of the thrill of the hunt—for myself, for my daughter and for you.

Section One:
New & Improved!

One

The Mother Lode:
The Promise of Products

Phyllis is with her mother and it is important. They are shopping for her wedding dress. Other times they've fought about what she could buy, what would look right, what would be appropriate. Once she took her babysitting money and snuck away with a friend to New Brunswick, N.J., to buy a chiffon dress for the church field trip. She wanted to choose it for herself, escaping her mother's taste, her mother's control. But this time is different. This time Phyllis seeks her mother's opinion.

"We've gone to bridal fairs, we've gone to boutiques, we've looked at all the magazines," says Phyllis, her hands clasped primly in her lap. "We're in a bridal shop in a Victorian house. I know what I want. I trust the salesperson. She owns the shop. She's the one who's bringing in all the accessories: crown, veil, shoes, bag.

"I feel she knows what goes together and I'm right! It is all perfect. She has good taste. She's recommending. It's going to be perfect. I just know it."

Phyllis stops talking. Her eyes have been and remain closed. She seems happy: happy to have found the right dress, happy to have experienced the memory, happy to have shared it. Her wedding was more than 20 years ago, but there in her mind's eye is the dress, fresh, perfect, new, now. There she is, Bridal Phyllis, ensconced in the reimagined muted gray, carpeted dressing room with the white lacquered, louvered wooden door and burnished brass door handle. She and her mother sit on plush mauve chairs, surrounded by mirrors, contemplating, discussing, choosing, anticipating.

An hour ago, Phyllis had been noticeably nervous as she sat down at the table. She had placed the tent card with her name in front of her, glanced quickly around, catching and immediately releasing her own gaze in the massive mirror that claims nearly an entire wall. She was not surprised by the fact of such a reflection; she has been in a focus group before, albeit not like this one. In this group, the women will be hypnotized.

She is a woman of a certain age and income, a college graduate and teacher, married with no children, but no one is inquiring about any of that. It has already been detailed in a telephone questionnaire and summarized on a sheet of paper. She has made the cut. Phyllis is someone to whom we want to listen.

A tall, slender woman, she wears a green leaf print cotton dress with a pale pink form-fitting jacket. Her blond hair is parted in the middle and curls softly in layers before turning up slightly at her shoulder, an aging homage to a youthful Farrah Fawcett. Her purse is placed under her chair. Her feet, as she's been told they should be, are flat on the floor.

She is not alone, of course. There are six other women around the table. Angie weeps to remember how youthful her mother looked when she helped Angie shop for her wedding dress, with its beads and ruffles and deeply debated veil. "She's so young," Angie sobs. "So young."

There is a man here, too: Hal Goldberg, who has hypnotized them. This is Hal's life. The mesmerizing world of the hypnosis focus group. Yesterday, he talked with men about beer; tomorrow he will talk with mothers of six-year-olds about presweetened breakfast cereal. Through each two-and-a-half-hour session, he calmly excavates memory, meaning and mayhem from the web of associations that filter our choices when we shop. And I sit on the other side of the mirror, eating too many peanut M&Ms and staring intently at consumers as though I am Jane Goodall and they are primates in the wild.

Hal's is a calm presence. His sandy hair is flecked with gray. He is carefully groomed in a sedate, deep brown pinstriped suit, minutely patterned beige and chocolate tie and clunky, if earnest, cordovan wingtips. His formality seems otherworldly in this suburban office park setting, where most women are more inclined than Phyllis to wear jogging suits or jeans with halter tops. Hal's demeanor induces serious serenity; his voice, the verbal equivalent of a neck massage.

"I want you to stare at the green dot above my head," he has told them. "I want your faces toward me, but your eyes on the green dot." Each time he hits his mark. Quietly shuffling the papers that hold his notes, he walks them back, into and through their memories. "Let your imaginations—lend me your imaginations—let your imaginations drift," he says, time and again, the stutter step of this exhortation replicated with precision, group after group, day after day, week after week, year after year. How can he do it so exactly the same? Is there some reason he does it this way? I have always wondered and never asked, any more than he asks me what I do with this information.

The women trust his soothing tone and relax. They follow his instruction to go down, down, down into the tranquil, bemused state he compares with "highway hypnosis," when they drive by their exits, minds aware but daydreaming.

"Has anybody here ever daydreamed? I think I spend half my life daydreaming," he shyly admits, as they smile. The same wee joke made in the same place in the script each time. Ah, yes. They are all in it together. They have all driven by their exits. Hal knows and understands.

Eyes flutter shut and, when he calmly explains their eyelids are the most relaxed muscles in their bodies, unable now to open even if they wanted, he is right. Their eyelids have been sealed; their memories opened.

For 30 minutes Hal drones on, taking them ever further into the peaceful realm from which they will each recall a first, a most powerful, and a most recent memory of shopping. He relaxes and regresses them to a place where the rigid boundaries between Now and Then release. He has not asked about buying wedding dresses; he has asked about their most memorable, most powerful shopping experience. Again and again it is the memory of buying the wedding dress that surfaces.

A detail emerges and it is crucial: They are speaking about wedding dress shopping in the present tense. I bolt upright. I realize they are really in the moment, experiencing this memory as if they are shopping right now. I lean forward, scribbling notes more quickly, trying to track every word. It is being videotaped so I can look at it later, but still. We don't always get a reaction at once this clear and this unvarying.

Hal questions each of them in turn. How did they feel when they found this perfect object of desire? They dutifully answer when called upon.

"It was fun. I felt it was the beginning of freedom," says Phyllis, eyes shut and seemingly focused on an inner TV screen.

"There was a wildness to it, independence," says Janice.

"We were having such fun," says Jenna. "It was pure."

"It was exciting!" says Rhonda. "I wasn't used to getting new clothes, but I felt it coming down my body as I tried it on and I knew it was right. My mother agreed. The saleslady wasn't sure, but my mother backed me up. It was thrilling."

Ah! The Wedding Dress. Sigmund Freud says all we want is significance. The elements of a woman's wedding day conspire to prove her significance and the process begins in earnest with the dress. "It mattered, it was important," says Janice. "Everything was swirling around me," says Phyllis. "It was just crucial to get the right one," says Rhonda.

It is the archetypal shopping experience, the Rosetta Stone for married women, whether happily married or not. It decodes everything. And, although money must have been a constraint, they never mention it. We are in a magical world, beyond price here.

Few shopping experiences live up to this expectation. But there it rests, the subconscious standard by which we judge every trip to every store. It makes sense to deconstruct it carefully. What are the criteria, the standards, the phases that each of these women describes? There is a common thread, a series of steps we must take to experience shopping nirvana. We hear them again and again: the four pulse points to the Ideal Shopping Experience. Together they transcend the essential "thinginess" of the thing acquired, reorient the shopper on her life's path and recast her relationships with everyone in the process.

It is through the work of this Ideal Shopping Experience that we forge our hope (and disappointment) for all shopping, seeking always the genuine *Shopportunity!* The first is **Anticipation.**

"I had looked forward to it for so long," Rhonda tells Hal. "I knew it the moment I saw it. I'd been planning it in my mind since I was seven."

"It was an event," says Julie. "It was fun because it was so exactly what I'd imagined and looked forward to. I felt so, so happy."

"I'm looking for my wedding dress. My mother is with me," says Jenna, the married mother of a three- and a six-year-old. "We're at The Bridal Sophisticate. I'm trying one on to be nice, because the salesgirl is helpful, but I know exactly what I want. I've seen it in a catalog. I show her the picture. She has it!

"My mother wonders if I'm not missing something. I don't want to try other dresses on. This is it. This is the one! I'm so excited. It's what I've dreamed about."

Indeed, in interview after interview it emerges that shopping for a wedding dress culminates years of expectation that began with little Rhonda's first viewing of *Cinderella* or *The Sound of Music.* The anticipation escalated through time, through Barbie and Ken play, through sleepless sleepovers with girlfriends talking into the night about seventh-grade crushes, through celebrity wedding voyeurism, through first dates, proms, through primping, pinning and pining, through breaking someone's heart and someone breaking ours, before ratcheting up to bridesmaid duty.

"I'd looked forward to it for so long," says Elaine. "Just so much anticipation since I was a little, little girl and now here we were, trying on my wedding dress. I felt like a princess, so happy, so excited."

Then, comes the **Pursuit**. In the case of a wedding dress, this is nothing less than the pursuit of perfection: Shopping for the wedding dress starts the process of making the wedding real.

It is Janice's turn. "I'm trying on my wedding dress," she tells Hal. "We're in an upscale place. My mother is with me. She's showing me the dresses and I don't like them. But when I see it, I know! It is what I've envisioned I'll wear. We're in Brides by Beatrice. It's what I've imagined: stately, elegant."

"My mother and I knew what we wanted," explains Elaine. "We just kept going from one shop to another, looking in magazine after magazine until we found it. It took months. But nothing else would do. We just kept on searching."

At last count, there are at least four bridal bibles in this country, *Bride's, Modern Bride, Martha Stewart Weddings* and *Bridal Guide,* all chockablock with thousands of pages of advertising each year. *Marrying at 20, 30 or 40! Perfect Dresses! Beauty Secrets! Real Couples! Expert Advice!* To this array add scores of gorgeous coffee table books, catalogs, bridal fairs, articles about the iconic weddings of the rich and famous and, of course, the personal fables of friends. All these experts provide the salient "how to" and "what to" advice to help the bride on her quest for wedding perfection.

Third is **Prominence.** Our culture treasures weddings, if not always marriage. If the bride is Queen for a Day, then the bridal gown shopper is Princess for the Duration. Luxurious fitting rooms, pile carpeting, offers of refreshment, enhanced lighting to make everyone glow like a lover, attentive staff, seamstresses at the ready to make alterations at sequential fittings, all whip around like Munchkins readying Dorothy for the Wizard, respectful of her wishes and eager to please. She's changed her mind? No problem. How about this? Or this? Maybe she'd like this?

Such prominence requires an avatar, the learned one to shepherd her through, putting her on that level playing field with her mother. Every Cinderella needs a fairy godmother and that role is performed by the trusted salesperson. She knows more, has seen more and brings more wisdom to bear on this particular bride's particular hopes.

"I feel so happy," says Phylis. "We're laughing, it feels so exciting. My mother, the saleslady, my best friend. There's such good energy in the dressing room. We're all so happy."

Fourth, along with Anticipation, Pursuit and Prominence,

every wedding dress comes ready to benefit from **Appreciation.** I'm borrowing a term from accounting to describe something beyond the fact that everyone tells a bride she's beautiful. I'm talking about a sense of enduring value. The dress appreciates over time as few purchases do. The wedding dress is put away, encased in its wardrobe bag. It may be brought out later to be viewed by children, foreshadowing their own call to romance. (At this moment, the children begin their own journey of anticipation.) Unlike T-shirts, workout gear or even prom dresses, it accumulates value with each elaboration on the telling of the tale. It may be worn again and maybe even again, gaining layers of meaning through family tradition, folklore and ritual. And with each wearing, it becomes more packed with emotional density and complexity. The dress becomes a totem of the woman we were and dreamed we'd become.

These four ingredients make the heady cocktail of a *Shopportunity!:* Anticipation, Pursuit, Prominence and Appreciation. Done right, the wedding dress packs a wallop. It is a potent rite moving a bride into the excitement of an emerging new life, fraught with hope and, yes, fear and trepidation. Shopping for the wedding dress is a transformational moment for the shopper at its heart. It recasts her relationship with nearly everyone she knows: father, lover, friends, family and particularly with her mother, who morphs in that moment into friend. Everything changes.

"My mother and I are deciding," Phyllis says. "We're like friends, like sisters. I feel my relationship with my mother changing. I want her opinion. My life is going to be better and different from now on."

For men the equivalently defining moment is buying their first car, usually with their father along, preparing to accede to their wishes with a tiny frisson of envy mixed with memory.

Just like the women in the focus groups, men respect the shock of recognition. They know what it will feel like to put key to ignition of their car, they know the relative merits of each exterior color—Olivine Green Metallic vs. Black Sapphire vs. Titanium Silver—and have imagined how each will correspond with the Dream Red and Black High-Performance Leather with Graphite Finish Interior Trim for which they lust. They have done their homework.

They have *anticipated* this moment for years, memorizing car grille details and identifying models from far off, reading *Car & Driver* and arguing the merits of various engines. They have taken driver's ed classes and studied for their license, dreaming of the cars they'd own, one day, when they were grown.

In *pursuit* of this vision, they have worked and saved to meet the challenges set by their fathers. "You make the down payment, I'll cosign the loan." "I'll put in $1,000, after that you're on your own." "You can have my old car, but you need to pass geometry with at least a C." "If you get into Harvard, I'll buy you a BMW." However high the bar, they have jumped.

The *prominence* that comes with possession will be theirs. They will be drivers, drivers of their own cars. They will be able to go anywhere and do anything, once the car is theirs. They know how people will look at them as they drive past, what their friends will say, what girls will think of them.

And, this experience *appreciates* over time. "Oh, that I'd kept that car and never sold it; just put it on blocks. What would it be worth today!" "I saw one just like it on eBay—and you know I could get it for $8,200." They will bring out the pictures from that first road trip to regale their children, and begin the anticipation cycle anew.

It is fun. It is excitement. It is independence. It is thrill.

It is shopping.

The project of this book is to prove that these transcendent shopping experiences are more attainable than we think. Not everyone has a Wedding Day Barbie dress or a Porsche Boxster for a first car, but we all carry within us the hope of finding what we need, when we need it—and of enjoying the process. Tragically we settle for much, much less, seduced by the shell game barked by con artists touting cheap, rather than holding out for the perfection of significance.

So the first rule of *Shopportunity!* must be to relearn anticipation: the fine art of looking forward to buying a truly special something. Let's buy neither from impulse nor boredom, but from authentic, legitimate, long-term desire. What if every dress were a wedding dress? Every car a first car? How we would study up on it, look forward to it, imagine our lives with it. And we would hunger to know its details, its nuances. We would long to care for it, preserve it and protect it—and how beside the point price would be. We would not buy much, but we would buy well. And oh! how we would shop.

Rule #1: Relearn Anticipation

"Ah, but I'm only buying laundry detergent," you say.

"Read on," I say.

Two

Getting the Promise to Market: Send Us More Floating Soap

Katherine Krueger pushes the hair away from her face. It is hot. North Dakota, August, 1920 hot. Nothing stirs the air. Dirt from the road rides on any errant breeze kicked up by horse-drawn carriage or Model T. She is wearing a Gibson Girl getup, issued by the hotel but taken care of by her: starched white blouse, long black gabardine skirt, high-button shoes. She's got a smock over her shirt, but knows she'll have to have a "sponge bath" and put on a new top before the dinner rush, if she's to look fresh for Walter.

Breakfast is over in the coffee shop and she is now going about the business of cleaning the rooms. This room in particular she doesn't mind cleaning. It belongs to Walter Hanson, the Soo-Line railroad man she waited on at breakfast. He was paid yesterday, the end of the month. She's searching for his paycheck and when she finds it on the bedside table she is dumbstruck. It is more money than her farmer father sees in a year, and yet it is for just two weeks' work. She will marry him.

Katherine is seduced not by his rough-hewn Norwegian looks but by the idea of living in town, in Drake. In town, she reasons, there will be relative ease compared to the well-known drudgery of the farm her father homesteads with her nine brothers. The farm is where she's grown up, living in a sod hut carved from the Dakota plains. Her mother died when she was ten and she dropped out of the one-room schoolhouse to take care of them all, plus the threshing crew each wheat harvest.

In town, she knows there will be only her and Walter to look after and he, after all, will be traveling. At some point, there will be children, but even that seems simple compared to the never-ending servitude on the farm.

Katherine is scrubbing the floor of Walter's room, on her hands and knees with a scrub bucket and an eight-inch brush with rounded edges to get into the corners. Sweat slithers from her forehead to chin to floor and infuses the sudsy slurry with one more drop to mop up. It is 102 degrees outside, probably 110 degrees in the airless room. She uses Fels Naphtha soap. She wants him to know she's a good housekeeper. She wants him to see that she knows what she's doing. She has already made the bed taut, fluffed the pillows and washed down the windowsill where the street grime settles, wafting in through the shutters.

She thinks of what it would be like to be married to a man with that much money. Katherine is pretty and a good dancer. She is known as "the belle of three counties." Another man has asked for her hand by explaining to her father than he has 10,000 bushels of grain in the silo, but she has vetoed it. "I'm marrying a man, not a silo." Still, it's time. She can't, she won't work at a hotel her whole life.

She dreams not of the wedding itself, but of the way she'll manage her household. Monday will be washing day. She will need a "day of rest" beforehand to be ready for it. She'll heat the water for the tub on the cookstove, using lye first on the stains, Fels Naphtha on collars and cuffs, swirling the clothes around in the hot froth, scrubbing his shirts and underclothes clean on the washboard, along with her own things, the towels, the sheets, then slurping them out and into first one rinse tub and then another, then through the wringer to force water from them, taking care not to let her fingers get caught in the wringer the way Aunt Viola's did. Wicker wash basket by wicker wash basket, she'll cart the waterlogged laundry down to the basement's dank coolness. Dinner on laundry day will be Sabbath leftovers, to save time and help her recover from the bruising exhaustion of the work.

She dreams on, now scrubbing down the floor at the corner by the window. When she has a little girl, she'll dress her all in white, so that everyone in town knows they have money and she's a good homemaker.

Fels Naphtha soap. She blesses Fels Naphtha soap.

She will not have to follow the ritual of soap making taught to her by her mother who learned it from her mother, using household waste products: bacon grease and the ashes of a wood fire. It was Katherine's first job as a child and she knows it well: melting and filtering the fat, rendering it pure, adding the potash to the bubbling stew, and stirring it for hours over the hot stove until it firms up like a gravy, then cooling it, adding salt, skimming the soap off the top of the goop, putting it into wooden molds and then aging it in the root cellar. Yes, Katherine blessed the day her father had said it was permissible to buy Fels Naphtha soap.

Tuesday will be ironing day. She'll heat two irons on the top of the cookstove, attaching the single wooden handle to each iron in turn, so there's always one to use until it cools, and one hot and at the ready. She'll wet the clothes with water from an old Coke bottle with a cork sprinkler in it. Walter will be pleased to know she can mix her own starch, believes that sheets and towels should be ironed and turns out a dress shirt better than any of her nine sisters-in-law. When the ironing basket overflows and the chore leaks into evening, Walter will come to sit near her in the kitchen, keeping her company, their conversations pulsed to the steady beat of iron on board.

Katherine is a good baker. Wednesday will be her favorite day. First she'll make the bread loaves and the cinnamon rolls, then, the doughnuts, the cakes, the strudels. She has won prizes at the county fair for her breads. The threshing crews loved her doughnuts, deep fried dough they'd come in midmorning to eat with coffee before returning to the fields. She will find a way to bring this into conversation tonight, when Walter comes into the coffee shop, hungry for dinner, for conversation.

Mending will be Thursday's event. The mending basket filled quickly in a home with ten men. She's learned to fix anything, rips and tears, missing buttons. She can alter hand-me-down pants, shirts and jackets as they migrate from one brother to the next. She can make dresses from scratch. Just looking at a picture in the Sears & Roebuck catalog somehow telegraphs the pattern to her hands and she goes to work. She taught herself to crochet, late at night when everyone else was asleep. As a ten-year-old with only the memory of a mother to guide her, she put a blanket under the doorjamb to her room so her father wouldn't see her wasting kerosene and she unraveled the dresses her mother crocheted, reversing the process in her mind and learning to rebuild the pattern, one stitch at a time.

She will be a good catch for Walter: He will love the pies she will bake on Friday and he will admire her ability to clean an entire house on Saturday, floor to ceiling, wainscoting and boot-muddied rungs of chairs, beating the carpets and giving everything a vicious scrub. She'll raise their children to know how to do it too. Katherine and Walter will marry. They will have three children, one of whom will become my mother and tell me these tales from rural America of the 1920s.

Exotic in my own childhood, Katherine's homespun tales of domestic drudgery and miraculous cleaning aids are baffling now. Is it really possible to make soap? At home? With what?

By 1920, Katherine was already a laggard in terms of her ability to embrace these products. They arrived decades earlier in urban areas, already commonplace along with the other mile markers of the emerging consumer society: electric lighting, indoor plumbing, central heating, iceboxes—and department stores. The transformation of this culture from production to consumption was essentially accomplished in 100 years, from 1860 to 1960. Household cleaning products were just one more signpost along the highway.

Arthur C. Clarke wrote, "Any sufficiently advanced technology is indistinguishable from magic." That statement may be equally applied to any sufficiently advanced category of product. The early years of the household cleaning products industry in this country illustrate the power of product magic. They heralded a profound Cultural Transformation—the point at which we move from *"if* I'm going to buy this type of product" to *"which* of these products will I buy."

In Katherine's day, household products like Fels Naphtha soap delivered the trifecta of product promises: I will transform your day, I will transform your life, I will transform your world. Transformation is the essential covenant brands make with us. Cultural transformation is what they sometimes deliver. It is fair to say that without the household cleaning product revolution, there could have been no women's movement. There would have been no time and little energy. It may have been an unanticipated outcome, but it's an outcome nonetheless.

Good soap was life altering. It returned hours to a day, days to a week and free time was the ultimate substantiation of upper-class status. Good soap, and its branded progeny, were in sync with the anticlassist, democratizing promise of the country itself. For millions of America's poor, struggling at the margins, the mainstream road of branded products was a path they could not afford to take. But for many more, for the emerging consumer market, the brand promise was straightforward: You can bridge the great class divide and live a life as leisurely, clean and ordered as the rich—and have beautiful hands into the bargain. You can be a loving, nurturing mother to your children—and perhaps pursue some interests of your own. The promise, aimed at the hearts and minds of women and through them to their families, was relief from drudgery for, well, if not all, then many, perhaps most.

The *sanctum sanctorum* for the world of household consumer products we inhabit today is a huge corporate structure in Cincinnati at what used to be Sixth and Sycamore and is now officially dubbed One and Two Procter & Gamble Plaza. What hath Harley Procter and James Gamble wrought? It was their fathers who, as candle and soap makers, joined forces in 1846. They could not have dreamed in their wildest flights of fancy (if candle and soap makers can be said to have had such things) the global enterprise their product formulas have conjured.

Today, P&G is a $60 billion company with four global divisions, operating on six continents. Its products touch consumers two billion times a day. Sixteen of its brands sell more than $1 billion per year each. We know them all: Tide, Bounce, Downy, Bounty, Charmin, Crest, Scope, Pampers, Always, Swiffer, Puffs, Head & Shoulders, Olay, Zest, Secret, Cascade, Joy, Dawn, Mr. Clean and first and not least, Ivory.

P&G pioneered the basic premise upon which consumer product marketing is based, via its Ivory brand of soap. Create a demonstrably superior product that responds to consumer needs and then market it supremely well.

This philosophy was not coined in the halls of academia. It is the by-product of wisdom earned the hard way by Harley Procter and James Gamble, seeking to make their mark on an already successful company. The duo's first breakthrough product was Ivory soap, meant to compete with the imported Castile soaps of the day. (That unique notch to cut the bar in half was designed to allow Ivory to be used both as a laundry and a toilet soap.) One day in 1879, legend has it, a plant worker left the soap mixer running while he went out to lunch. He came back, noticed the mistake and, figuring nothing bad had happened, processed that batch, packaged it and shipped it out.

Soon enough, letters came in to the company begging them, "Send us more floating soap." At that time, along the Ohio River, women were washing themselves and their families in brackish river and well water; a soap that could float to the top of the tub meant a lot.

Ergo: Respond to consumer needs.

Procter also wanted to be able to make claims for the product that could be substantiated by more than "because we say so." He sent his floating soap off to a lab in New York and asked them to analyze it. He got back a report that said that there were .56 percent miscellaneous particles in it. Thus was born the phrase: "99.44 percent pure: It Floats."

Ergo: Create a *demonstrably* superior product.

Procter was the partner who was more interested in marketing. He'd learned the value of branding when he shipped his wooden cases of product down the Ohio River: It helped to burn a mark on the side of the boxes (like branding cattle), so that store owners would know the products in the boxes came from him. The moon and stars logo was fashioned from the inherently functional laborers' marks on the sides of the crates.

He reasoned branding the products inside could help as well. Thus, the emergence of brand names, like Ivory. And rather than rely solely on store owners to sell his product, he mounted the first national advertising campaign by commissioning respected artists to illustrate the value of using Ivory. He placed these remarkable ads in the pages of respected national women's publications of the time, creating mass consumer demand. For the first time, Katherine walked into Gus Janavarus's general store in Drake, North Dakota and demanded a specific brand, advertising tear sheet in hand.

Ergo: Market it supremely well.

Our grandmothers and great-grandmothers surely didn't know the name of the company or the men behind it, but they must have sensed a mighty train was leaving the station and they scurried aboard. P&G products worked in lockstep with the evolution of consumer appliances, such as the washing machine, the steam iron, the refrigerator, the clothes dryer and the dishwasher. If Thomas Edison's electricity replaced labor with current, the P&G products served as the transformer, supplanting elbow grease and time with a dazzling array of goods designed for a specific purpose, all colluding to make a dirty house into a clean, well-managed and maintained home.

To be clear, the washing machine that was developed and marketed in the 1930s and 1940s simply could not have taken hold of our homes as it did had it not been for P&G's relentless and successful pursuit of detergent chemistry, which finally bore fruit in 1938 with Tide. Women wanted convenience, of course, but not at the expense of clean. And Tide gave them clean, conveniently— and cleanly better than anything they'd seen before.

And it gave them a meaningful memory trace, a pathway back to the ideal of clean, through aroma. As one brand manager told me, "If your mother used Tide, nothing else smells like clean."

•   •   •

If the chores were female-centric, and they were, then the choice of which products and brands would obliterate them became the new women's work, while the labor each purchase required fell on men like Walter to provide. Today, most marketers acknowledge 80 percent of all purchases are made by women, regardless of who ultimately uses the product.

The expression "homemade," which was once a term of praise, became cause for apology. Yes, of course, some women still "make from scratch," but they are clearly the exceptions that prove the rule. We may worship at the altar of homemade, but all we have the time, perhaps talent, perhaps inclination to do, as Duncan Hines so presciently understood, is put the egg into the cake mix. We began to replace the *doing* of the task—whether cooking, sewing or cleaning—with talking and reading about the task in the score of women's journals that emerged to dispense advice.

Why? Despite the change in how women spend their time, and despite their enormous relief from drudgery, the *wish* still lingers that they could make soap from scratch, no matter how backbreaking the process might be. Thus, the "homemaking voyeurism" of Martha Stewart pervades. We may not actually want to do it, but it is thrilling to know that someone knows how to and is willing, motherlike, to show us.

The mother wish lingers in our collective unconscious. Martha simply channeled the yearning to ground. Mother can, if not actually *do* all these things, cause them to be done: Clean clothes arrive in the closet, food appears in the pantry, the cookies await our return from school. Our mother, through packaged totems, loves us and cares for us. The role formerly performed by Mother will now be understudied by a host of helpers; the homemaker mother genie is out of the bottle and will not go back. The culture is transformed.

Procter & Gamble knows that it is the aroma of coffee that seduces us. It telegraphs that "Mom's in the kitchen, all's right with the world" and pulls us unconsciously toward it, seeking that blanketing nurture we recall from countless winter mornings, when the best part of waking up was the smell of Folgers in our mother's percolator. Nabisco knows that wrapped within every packaged sweet baked treat is the idea that "my mother loves me," encoded there from after school and lunchbox treats that seemed like a veritable kiss themselves.

Today, the appeal of a packaged consumer product rests often on its ability to imitate the archetypal mother. One hypothesis states we love packages that mimic the very first package we touched: Mother's breast. Look at the "nipples" on bottled water bottles. Consider the allure of the POM bottle packaging. We long for liquids that arrive so enshrined. How much more could P ♥ M look like MOM?

The cultural shift to women as editors of—rather than makers of—the home began at the expense of men, or at least of their paychecks, of course. But I do not mean to suggest that it was an unalloyed boon to women. There was a toll exacted. Betty Friedan thought of it as "the problem that has no name," this disenfranchisement from the kind of productive work valued by society, this morphing into consumers of other people's work.

Shopping, at its worst, then becomes simply one more rote chore, the goal of which is to beat the system, via counterfeit couture, double coupons, and buy-one-get-one-free deals. It morphs into a love/hate exercise signaling profound consumer ambivalence. Thus, we're glad we don't contemplate the grinding realities that Katherine did, but at the same time we prefer our packaging in the shape of a nipple. Shopping becomes as incoherent as a mood swing. Sometimes it seems like a "mini trip to Las Vegas," with surprises and delights along the way; sometimes, it's more like the aftermath of too much time spent at the slots, with only buyer's remorse to show for it.

The moment was a transitory one, but should be marked: Housework was once contingent upon the labor of women. It alchemically transformed somewhere in early 20th-century America into the selection process, choosing among competing brands. Women became the shop stewards of labor-saving products and devices, all designed to free them from the time and talent it takes to make your own soap, starch, bread—from the grinding reality of housework.

Of course, within 20 years of that initial freedom, women entered the then-male sphere of out-of-home work, in order to fund, in part, this emerging convenience habit. Women traded one type of work for another, at once more engaging, more frustrating, certainly more guilt producing at least at it relates to raising children and, sometimes, more financially rewarding than our grandmothers envisioned. But always the project of homemaking remains part of woman's role, now often reconstructed as the work of budget management.

"Blue-collar workers tend to like to shop in hostile or difficult environments like Wal*Mart because that has become the work of homemaking," explains Brett Stover, vice president of consulting and global shopping expert for Glendinning Management Consultants, a WPP company. "For a lot of housewives, a big part of the contribution to the family and to their identity as women is saving money. Wal*Mart allows them to do that in adverse conditions. Coping and occasionally triumphing over that adversity is the work they do."

And so we arrive here, without quite understanding where we are. The cultural transformations wrought by consumer products are powerful, but the basic laws of physics do apply: Every action has an equal and opposite reaction. We have traded an ability to do things for the ability to get things done.

I am struck with Cheryl Mendelson's ode to the lost sensory pleasures of laundry day: "It's sensually pleasing, with its snowy, sweet-smelling suds, warm water and lovely look and feel of fabric folded or ironed, smooth and gleaming." Referring to the time she moved at 13 to suburbia she tells the *New York Times:* "My whole identity was erased. Here I'd grown up doing laundry in the backyard, hanging it on the line with my grandmother. Then I get to suburban America and all this was regarded with complete contempt. Other mothers were saying things like, 'I don't want you to know about these things—you're going to be something.' "

We have gained a better, brighter, whiter, antibacterial suffused cleanliness. We have gained the ability to relish the occasional trophy dinner, with designer ingredients, perfectly paired wines, and gorgeous table settings. We have gained the time to do things we want to do more than we want to clean and cook and then clean and cook all over again.

We have forfeited the quiver of daily elation, whether in the laundry room or at the nightly family dinner table. We have lost personal human contact with our grocer, becoming a transaction to him, while to us "he" has become an "it," a nameless hostile combatant in an enemy minefield we must fight our way through and out of, as quickly as possible. We have lost the enchantment of small triumphs.

"Women are constantly torn between the desire to make a home beautiful and to escape it," writes Gail Collins. Precisely.

The ultimate promise of Fels Naphtha soap, Ivory, Tide and, hey, even Walter, was the cultural liberation of women from the drudgery of housework. But the open question was, to what greater purpose? I grew up on those secondhand tales of Katherine's washing day and laundry day. I witnessed firsthand my mother's liberation through the advance of time-saving, labor-saving consumer home products.

Products make promises and the brands frame those promises for us in ways we can emotionally connect to, but it is the products that have this magical DNA, the power to move an entire culture from one plateau to another vista. With household cleaning products, the promise was sheer magic, and the immediate beneficiaries of this magic were women like Katherine.

If the first rule of *Shopportunity!* is to "relearn the fine art of looking forward," then the second is to enjoy the choices. When presented with Fels Naphtha, or floating soap or detergent, women like Katherine recognized the benefits immediately. They made room in Depression-era budgets to get this new kind of clean. They wanted and got more floating soap, and a great deal more. Katherine and millions of women like her, through their intimate, personal product decisions, moved a culture. The culture having moved, moved on.

Rule #2: Enjoy Your Choices

And so must we. Time to consider that brands must evolve and grow with us—or be shed.

Three

Shedding One Skin and Forging Another, Brand by Brand

W e are not unlike a particularly hardy crustacean," writes Gail Sheehy in her still startling book, *Passages.* "The lobster grows by developing and shedding a series of hard, protective shells. Each time it expands from within, the confining shell must be sloughed off. It is left exposed and vulnerable until, in time, a new covering grows to replace the old. With each passage from one stage of human growth to the next, we, too, must shed a protective structure."

This world view tells us a great deal about our relationship to the products we use and the brands we choose. Every seven years or so, our lives do change and a window into new products and brand relationships opens. Life-stage marketing is a well-defined science, by this point. Two elements of it, however, are not so well understood: One, the seven-year, predictable cycle of it, as we move from one Sheehy-tracked life stage to the next, and two, the permission we grant brands to grow with us, even to shepherd us, as we reach each new transition.

Consider the newborn. Wanting only such food, warmth and shelter as he's been so recently ripped from, he is innocent of other expectation and therefore innocent of other disappointments. His cries can be pretty easily assuaged. Slowly, he discovers his incipient individuality: No to creamed spinach. Yes to footed pajamas.

These likes and dislikes swirl around in the relatively circumscribed world of his mother's choices, until somewhere around six or seven. Then comes that first serious interaction with someone else's mother or family. Perhaps it's a first sleepover or a truly extended play date, but some away-from-mother moment launches a cascade of epiphanies. We use Crest, but Laurie's family uses Colgate. We watch Disney, but Jeffrey's mom says he can watch Cartoon Channel. We got Froot Loops at Nicholas's house and we never get them here!

Welcome to the next phase, childhood from 7 to 14, with its endless small and large negotiations, all tiny cries for a measure of independence and autonomy. Life beyond Cheerios seems a smaller struggle and Mom can't fight the war on every front, so she gives on Froot Loops, but demands schoolwork be done before television is watched. The triumph that brings Cocoa Puffs through the door becomes mere memory as tomorrow's skirmish over wardrobe, computer usage, or bedtime lurches into view.

And then comes high school, with its new kids, new rituals of coolness, new ways of fitting in, all arriving just as parents begin to become dumber and dumber. Oh, the misfortune of it. The indignity. The wardrobe misunderstandings, the haircut fights, the endless orneriness in nearly every topic. Why can't he have the North Face jacket that is *de rigueur* this winter? The other guys have Slvr phones. Cool kids drink Mountain Dew, not Diet Coke, Mommmmm.

At the cusp of adulthood, somewhere around 21, we hit it again. Whether it's the engagement with our first job, first apartment, first serious romantic interest, we begin trimming our preferences to jibe with new prevailing winds. We drink what our boss drinks, smoke what our boyfriend smokes, shop where our friends shop, read the newspaper and magazines they read, and seek to declare our emerging adulthood through the shorthand of brand tropes.

At 27, or thereabouts, we're making a new series of purchase and therefore brand decisions. Perhaps it's sparked by our wedding and setting up a real home, perhaps by a job promotion, but we take our next step forward and make new brand choices as a consequence.

LIFE-STAGE MARKETING PASSAGES

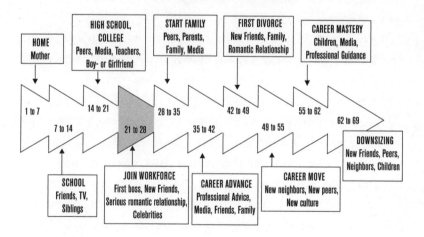

"As our life goals shift, our relationships must adjust, as well," explains Barbara Rothberg, Ph.D., a family therapist from Park Slope in Brooklyn, New York. "Life goals are malleable, progressive. A cereal brand that worked for us as a child won't align with our emerging identity as an adolescent."

Thus, the brands we seek to use to establish our young adult personality are necessarily badges borrowed from the adult world. Our brand relationships are every bit as mutable as our personal ones. We outgrow friends and sometimes spouses if their life goals aren't in sync with ours. Just as surely, we outgrow one series of brand choices to move on to the next.

Of the ten life stages I've documented, the coming of age transformation is often the most anxiety producing. The portal into adulthood requires nothing less than a formal cultural "coming of age" ceremony to enter.

Becoming adult is certainly not our only rough passage. There's birth, marriage and death, all ripe with meaning and ceremony. But coming of age takes the individual beyond the personal and bonds them to their culture at large. It's a moment worth lingering on. We are expanding into new roles. There are larger responsibilities and privileges, of course, with new rules to learn, new wisdom to gain, new risks to survive.

When Apache Indian girls came of age, the young woman sat in a hut for four days to mark her first menstruation. It was a ritual designed to allow the girls to gain the essence of White Painted Woman, the Apache's first woman.

Boys in Mali are brought into manhood through a series of stages, requiring several years. It is a process designed to entirely transform the child to man and from there to immortality.

The Diola, of southwestern Senegal, mark manhood at fifteen-to thirty-year intervals. An elder playing a sacred drum announces the time has come and the young man's male relatives shave the initiate's head. After ceremonial dancing and song, there is a trip to a sacred grove several hundred yards from the village for ritual circumcision. Only then are the young men allowed to begin the process of learning the responsibilities of adulthood.

In short, human social cultures typically employ a rite of passage which is fraught with danger and completed profoundly, unutterably alone in order to move the individual into a larger role in his or her community. In a consumer culture, one of the crucial ways we mark our transformations is through products. Our personal choice of a specific brand serves to signal the rest of the world where we are in our journey.

Our children become adults one at a time, surrounded by dangers. The difference is that ours come in packages: Liquor, tobacco, cars, drugs and even coffee are all rite-of-passage products that indoctrinate us into the "adults only" world of sophistication, power or independence. The desire to be fully adult, with its perceived power and its known dangers, propels us forward into the realm of products which, at least at first blush, are tough to like. Yet we learn to, because we yearn to.

Rite-of-passage products sit on two ever-shifting tectonic plates of safety and danger: the safety of doing what the culture espouses and the danger of learning to like products that we know in our hearts and minds have the power to do terrible things to us and through us. Rite-of-passage products enthrall us with evocative brand imagery, helping us tell ourselves and others who we exactly, precisely are.

Automobiles are among the most evocative transformational purchases; they resonate at so many emotional levels. There's clearly been a cultural transformation wrought by cars, as there was by floating soap. But buying a car is so much more than the binary "yes" or "no" of "Do you drive?" It is a potent symbol of adulthood. Right at the cutting edge of growing up—when we are "yeasty and embryonic" in Sheehy's terms—we pursue the ironclad identity provided by a Chevy, VW Bug, Scion or used BMW. And, of course, there is the personal mood elevation that comes with driving the open road: the fusion of automobile and autonomy.

Beyond that, however, a car is a rite of personal passage whether it is our first car or our tenth. Certainly a shiny new Jaguar signals to ourselves and our friends that we have arrived at a time when we can now afford it. From muscle car to minivan and back again, our choice of car earmarks our life-stage progression. And yes, a bright red, two-seater sports car can scream for us "I'm not getting older, I'm not, I'm not! I won't, I won't!" But it is that first car that sets the stage for all our future car choices. The first car shows us the transformational power of the automobile, its ability to provide us a glossy new "protective shell" of our emerging personality to better reflect to ourselves and others our budding persona. No wonder car makers obsess about that first car—nearly as much as we do.

"We started with a mission of giving 20-somethings a new car experience, like we'd done with their parents 30 years before," explains Matthew Gonzalez, head of strategy for Toyota, speaking about the amazingly successful launch of the Scion. "We wanted to invent a brand, as we'd done with Toyota, a generation earlier in this country. It needed to be affordable and different from their parents' car."

How did they do it? Few launch stories chart the highways and byways of shopper and marketspace realities as well as Scion. In order to create a new, hot nameplate, Toyota faced its own life-stage challenge. It needed to distance itself from its initial success. First-time car buyers wanted their own adventure, not their "father's Oldsmobile," or mother's Toyota, for that matter. Second, car dealers throughout the country were not eager to invest in a new dealership, spending money on real estate, inventory, sales staff and four-color brochures to dicker on price with kids for a $15,000 low-margin car. But without car dealers, the brand would stall.

Toyota's decision was to create a new brand, Scion. Then, they figured out there was a shared need between 20-something car shoppers and savvy, bottom-line driven dealers. According to Gonzalez, "We created the deep customization of Scion in order to respond to a young adult need we saw in the marketplace, and to show dealers how they could make money on the car."

Scion leaves many important choices up to the customer. Inside: Want a molded dash appliqué? How about a center armrest? Perhaps you'd like to have LED illumination: Yes or no. Up to you. Want to have a shift knob by OBX Racing Sports? Yes? Well, what color? Red, blue, chrome, gray. And hey! What color steering wheel? Gray? Red? Your call. Outside: Want to have real taillights by TYC? A custom-fit car cover, a rear bumper appliqué, any body side graphics (you've got seven to choose from, including the witty thumbprint, which is such an icon of the whole adventure). License plate frame? You've got three to choose from. Under the hood? Thinking maybe TRD struts and shocks would be nice, or a sport muffler, or lowering springs, or a quick shifter, or, or, or . . . maybe six- or eight- or 10-spoke wheel covers? Then, let's think about your personal sound system, right down to whether or not you want to cradle your iPod within.

When Gonzales speaks of "deep customization," he means it. Thrilling to the neophyte ready to show his or her parents a thing or two about car buying, it is equally gratifying to the dealer. "It may be a $15K car," he explains, "but with the customization options—which are sold by the dealers at a terrific margin—they can make as much on a Scion as they do a $20K car and it's more relevant for the buyer. This becomes 'my car,' unlike any other on the road."

Moreover, this mutual interest in customizing a car generates a genuine mentoring relationship. Neither one notices, perhaps, but it strikes an important note in the song of shopping. We need a coach, an honest broker, and here the buyer and seller become partners in the process, engaged in the project of pursuing their own interests, while serving each other's.

Shopportunity! perfected. The kid buys a new car and becomes an adult, mentored by a car salesman eager to provide him with precisely what he wants, a badge of individual personality. Life stage: Check. Then he drives his cultural ideal home. But the ride's not over. Each time key finds ignition there is a ripple of hope, of the open road, of exhilaration, of daring, of adventure. Check. This ongoing benefit, beyond the purchase epiphany, supplies the powerful continuing Appreciation that invests the car purchase with such meaning beyond the new car smell and admiring gaze of neighbors. This hit is of pure mood alteration: Check.

Nihar Patel, business strategy manager of Ford Asia Pacific and Africa, further explains, "Toyota did it right. There's no question. And it sits on an insight they gleaned in Japan, where space is tight and many young people have to live at home with their parents. The boxy design of the Scion suggests a home on wheels. It became the kids' space to make their own. It sits on a rich vein and I suspect they were surprised that it worked so well in America."

Gonzales agrees. "We thought the SA with its more conventional look would be the volume car and the SB, known as 'the box,' would go away in two years, because it was 'too far' out there, but that has not been the case. It's become such a signal that 'I'm doing my own thing in my own space.' Before first apartment, first home, comes first car I decorate myself. And we support that.

"We telegraph our content via our context. We use no mass media. Everything we do is about the discovery factor. We even work with the dealerships to ensure that there aren't 35 Scions on the lot—maybe just four or five. You may have to wait to get the exact car you want, but it's bespoke; it's yours and no one else's."

Clearly not all purchases are as heavy-laden. But the markers of maturity are acquired in the greater and lesser detail of our brand choices. Consider your morning coffee ritual. Once it meant you were growing up, you were acquiring a taste for a culturally correct product. Then it became usual, but your own profoundly personal ritual. Always it helps you undergo a daily change in mood, typically from asleep to awake, but sometimes from alone to in sync with a community of other coffee lovers, or from stuck on a work project to reinvigorated.

Procter & Gamble first identified the deep meaning of the rite of passage conveyed by coffee with Folgers, perhaps 20 years ago or more. It came at a time when coffee producers in general were wringing their hands in dismay that young people were no longer drinking coffee. Students had learned to get their "stay-awake-to-study-for-finals" caffeine from Coke and Pepsi.

The Coffee Council of America created an advertising campaign called Coffee Achievers, trying to convince young people that in order to achieve their goals in life, they needed to learn to enjoy coffee. The campaign failed, because it promised a benefit—personal achievement and success—that seemed well beyond the capability of a cup of coffee to deliver. It violated simple common sense. Coffee producers then defaulted to another age-old strategy. They attempted to cost-cut their way to growth, by using ever cheaper beans in order to ensure affordability for homemakers and profit for the 25-cent-a-cup coffee shop business. The coffee just kept tasting worse.

Procter & Gamble tried a radically different approach. The company hired Dr. Clotaire Rapaille, a charming, articulate anthropologist and psychiatrist. He argues that given a struggle among the cortex, the limbic and the reptilian sections of the brain, "The reptilian always wins." He believes fervently that consumers respond to certain products in their oldest, instinctive reptilian brain.

With the knowledge of a product's reptilian imprint, marketers can improve products and communication to better deliver on that essential promise. Rapaille believes consumers experience a "gut-check" rather than seek a rationale. Only later do they reframe their decision, using an "intellectual alibi."

His basic approach entails the ever tougher goal of getting people to simply calm down from the frenetic pace of daily life, to get in touch with their memories and their hopes and then to write down their brand or product stories. He works to find the structure behind the stories, in order to surface the "Code," which is what the brand actually stands for in the psyche of its users, and the "Cue," which is the sensory signal that alerts them they're actually getting what they're looking for from the brand.

What is our first memory of coffee? It is probably that moment in your childhood bedroom when the aroma of fresh brewed coffee wakes you up. Your most memorable cup of coffee was that first taste—which was nothing if not shocking. And your most recent memory is somewhere in between, whether it was the tepid vending machine version defaulted to on a late night at the office or a strong, pungent jolt of Starbucks.

Folgers' core insight was straightforward: The code for coffee is Home and the cue is Aroma. In other words, the damn stuff better smell good or you'll violate the covenant between psyche and brand. If the manufacturer gets the aroma right, you are teleported back to a warm toasty bedroom with visions of French toast dancing in your head.

In order to recapture that powerful promise, Folgers first reformulated the coffee, selecting ever more aromatic beans and investing in quality. Sure enough, the coffee smelled and tasted better, because it was made from superior, more expensive raw ingredients. Then, P&G created new packaging, with a patented vacuum seal that released the aroma with a purchase-ratifying whoosh. Now, we get a sound effect to help teleportation. Next, a resealable plastic lid that helped retain the freshness, the aroma—and the whoosh—every time we open it up.

Then and only then did Folgers apply the power of the cultural archetype to its advertising with a commercial that has aired for nearly two decades. In it, a young soldier comes home from the service by train at Christmastime. He sneaks into the house while his mother sleeps upstairs. We see him put the coffee on and the camera follows the aroma rising up to the mother's bedroom. She wakes to the smell and we watch the words "He's home!" form on her lips.

The commercial in this case evokes a significant transformation: the child smelling the coffee Mom made each morning. P&G and its agency reversed the archetype, child catering to parent, helping viewers claim for themselves that new identity of adult brewer and consumer of the coffee. The brand is there to help shepherd us through and mark the moment in which we first engage in this essential adult ritual.

Never mind that most of us gagged our first time over our first sip of coffee. Gagging precisely marks the moment of transformation. Important things are difficult. They happen to us alone. You'd think the promise of the brand would sputter out as we sputter like children. You'd think we'd say forget about adulthood, when we get a first taste of it. But no, there is a goal worth achieving. We push on, trying again. Since Folgers nearly killed us, but didn't, we stick with it. Folgers stuck with us, after all, at this precarious moment. Safety (Home) and Danger (the lure of an aroma that makes us gag), complete.

Howard Schultz of Starbucks must have had this same realization. That's why all the chairs are so comfy and living room–like: You're home. Not your old home and not your new home. You're in EveryHome. Walk into a Starbucks and you're confronted by the thrusting first shock of its specific, some say "burned," coffee aroma, then shepherded by your seduced senses into a homelike world away from home.

The smell of coffee is the trumpet's herald announcing you're safe in what Schultz calls the Third Space, but which we know to be a new home. You have to go to work and you have to go home, but this, this is where you *want* to go. The *baristas* are there to help you learn the language, reinvent your personal ritual and, most important, to help you belong.

There are other products that mark the dangerous passage into adulthood and carry a distinctly male mentorship aura. Cigarettes, of course, their essential *danger* acknowledged by historic icons who used them: cowboys and soldiers. While the first puff is clearly never as charming or sophisticated as the promise, the acquisition of the habit, a potent adult ritual, badges the smoker as a "Marlboro Man," "Camel Guy" or "Virginia Slims" suffragette. As with coffee, the powerful memory trace is established through opposition, and the promised transformation is sufficiently heady to create the psychic urge to tough it out and acquire the taste.

Cigarettes too take us from asleep to awake; that first cigarette in the morning is a reason unto itself for rising for smokers. But it also takes us from alone to engaged; once we've joined the club, there are others there. On a cigarette break when we bond with others similarly expelled from general society, the ubiquitous introductory mantra, "Got a light?" serves to telegraph a shared ritual, involving fire, danger and deep breathing. We use them to mark time, as an alternative to our watch, pacing our walk from the bus to our office, the commute from home to movie theater in seven-minute increments.

Smokers almost invariably refer to their pack of cigarettes as "my little friend," and so do cell phone users. While there's plenty of evidence to suggest that cigarettes are losing their toehold on cultural relevance, they seem still to operate both as a marker of adulthood and to elevate the mood of smokers. But for truly potent product experiences we need the trifecta of product promises; something able to fulfill the three-part transforming function (culture, life stage, mood) must come into play.

Sure enough, a quick glance down any urban street makes clear that the role formerly almost solely performed by a cigarette—keeping us company, connecting us with the larger society and badging us as a member of a certain part of the smoking society—is now being played by our mobile devices. We really cannot seem to go anywhere without them. We furtively sneak usage when we're told we cannot use them on an airline, in a movie or theater. We're not really sure that they might not be bad for us, after all. Kids, of course, lust after them particularly; witness the edgy attitude of Virgin Mobile as it seeks to bond early and often with these shoppers.

Every life stage has its own markers and they come alive through the mind's Reticular Activity Device. It's best explained anecdotally. When you buy the new car, you're amazed to realize how many others of that model are on the road, and how exciting it is to read an advertisement for the car you just bought. Or, when you have a child, you're overwhelmed by how many other children there are out there. It's an emergence of a new vision of the world, that's been opened by the portal you've just passed through.

An interview with a brand new father in the *New York Times* exemplifies this phenomenon: "The moment I saw the baby's head appear I was in awe," said [James] Joyce, 33, an executive in an interactive television company. "When I held him I felt overwhelming love rush all over me. I could feel the warmth on my chest—his skin on my skin. There's everything before. And everything after."

That's the moment that brands help us through. There's Before, as we shed our "hard-charging executive" armor. There's After, skin to skin, as we begin the acquisition of our fatherness. And right there, in that naked, fragile place is the precious marketing moment: We want information. We need information. We crave information. And through that information, transformation.

As another P&G brand manager told me about Pampers: "We know that there is only one woman who will pay attention to our message. She's in the third trimester of her first pregnancy or has fewer than two diaper-aged children at home." That's the moment she is reading, readying and really involved in becoming the mother she will be. She's eager for the information; the brand must step up and give it to her.

So, the third rule of *Shopportunity!* is to go ahead and let brands help us. They lend a hand through times of personal transformation. They move us daily from asleep to awake, and at key passages from single overachiever to reoriented parent, from soccer mom to empty-nester. When you give up your minivan to buy a luxury sedan, you declare to yourself and the world that you're no longer in the child-moving business. It's the "unadvertised special" available in many brands. They help us become who we imagine ourselves to be becoming.

Rule #3: Let Brands Transform You

Ready for a drink? Me too. Onward to mood transforming products and brands.

Four

The Brand Must Mean, Not Just Be

These adolescent males are not jocks. They are not hovering around the soccer field, not lifting weights in the gym, not even sitting on the bench during a high school baseball practice. They have no interest in Gatorade Culture. They are, in fact, more drawn to a 7-Eleven parking lot, or a video arcade. They are, despite the gravity defying, jailhouse chic of their jeans and scruffy stocking caps, the emerging technorati of their peer group. Indeed, their parents may nag them a bit about how much time they spend playing games on the Internet, but they are also the "go to" guys when it's time to connect the new printer or load the software.

These teen boys are not drinking Coke. They are not drinking designer bottled waters. They have outgrown Slurpees. These young men "Do the Dew." In fact, they are pretty much responsible for the radical success of Mountain Dew over the past decade, and, in particular, for the dazzling triumph of one varietal: Code Red.

"With Code Red, we realized that our appeal was to these guys who went to convenience stores and loved playing games on the Internet," says Cie Nicholson, chief marketing officer of PepsiCo now and the architect of the Code Red brand. "We knew it was about naming and framing this new product correctly and not overexplaining ourselves."

Truth be told, had it been more conventionally introduced, it might well have launched as "Cherry Mountain Dew," because that's what it is. Nicholson and her crew, however, got it right: They named it Code Red and never explained why. It just sounded cool. They put banner ads on the Internet that simply said, "Code Red is coming." Excitement began to mount, whatever Code Red was.

The beverage industry is a tough one. Brands may be developed, formulated and marketed by the corporation, but bottlers control the distribution. And bottlers are used to multimillion-dollar advertising campaigns to launch new brands, some introduced with Las Vegas–style razzle-dazzle at national bottlers' meetings. Exciting a bottler is high stakes poker: Every new product raises the ante, attempting to outdo the ones before. Before such a weathered group, Nicholson & Co.'s unconventional playbook must have seemed, well, less like innovation and more like desperation, or at least a lack of corporate commitment.

"After the 'teaser' campaign saying that Code Red was coming, we entered the next phase of our launch, putting a Code Red game on our Website," she recalls. "It attracted the core enthusiast, the guys who were already visiting our Website and decided to play the game. We promised the highest thousand scorers that we'd bring them two cases of the product, right to their door, when it became available, without ever telling them anything about the product."

It turned out that thousands upon thousands of teens, primarily males, played the game a staggering amount and earned high scores. So Nicholson bent the rules a bit, and awarded the top-scoring 1,500 the two cases. Imagine the moment when the delivery guy pulled up and delivered two cases of Code Red to their homes. The brand group waited to see what would happen as these first 3,000 cases were unleashed into the universe. The teens started taking two bottles of Code Red with them each day, one for themselves and one for "the cool kid." After all, they had Code Red and nobody else did. It became the ultimate *Shopportunity!*—the quest for an elusive, evocative elixir.

There was no television advertising for the first six months, to allow the young men to learn about the product and try it. Within a year it was a 100-million-case brand. Teens discovered it in 20-ounce single-serve sizes at the C-stores, but pretty soon their mothers were begging their grocery stores, and the grocery stores were begging the bottlers and the brand: Send us more Code Red!

"We knew teens wanted excitement in the beverage category," says Nicholson. "We wanted them to be able to have that thrill, without leaving the brand. We try to manage the excitement that's inherent in scarcity, too. Sometimes there's such demand that the store runs out. We're willing to accept that within a certain zone. We're willing to be interesting, but not irritating."

The Code Red approach was, I suspect, inspired by the world of the electronic games industry: Discovery Marketing, where the consumer does the work of driving demand. The playbook for game launches is a perfect illustration of how savvy companies conscript customers to market the product. Marketers focus on a young, smart, critical, loosely connected but highly communicative cell of hard-core enthusiasts.

"Serious gamers aren't stupid," explains Creed O'Hanlon,

founder of Spike.com and an Internet marketing guru. "They know more about the business than some game companies' CEOs, but they're happy to be complicit in it because they sense an understanding, maybe even a respect from the guys who want them to play and promote their games."

Why are teens willing to not only "Do the Dew," but to tell others to, too? How is it that *who* uses the brand becomes as important as *what* the brand does? The benefit it delivers to drinkers grows beyond the functional performance of the brew. It is about a social connection, the gaining of a witness to our life choices, and the significance of affecting others with our choices.

Importantly the brand at this point becomes the conduit of meaning. The brand isn't just the product, it is the meaning that both I and my culture attribute to it. It is the language through which such meaning moves.

When Hasbro, the toy company, gets ready to introduce a new toy or game, researchers go to the schoolyard and ask the first child they see who is the right age for the product, "Who is the cool kid in your class?" The child tells them, and they go to that youngster and ask the same question, and on and on until they come upon the child who says, "I am." That is the person to whom they give the toy or game to take home, try and report back about. They seek to create a sort of "breeder reactor" of enthusiasm about the new product, from which to jump-start its success.

Similarly, when Tylenol discovered that the entire 20-something audience had an attitude toward pain different from their parents, the brand began to consider the specter of losing an entire generation that was supremely uninterested in "taking comfort from our strength." Tylenol turned to my alma mater, Faith Popcorn's BrainReserve, to help them connect with these folks in a resonant way.

"Our research showed that young adults have a very different relationship to pain than any other generation," Popcorn recounted in an interview for this book. "They are not looking to avoid it: They actually like to claim it. They go out Rollerblading or windsurfing or mountain biking on the weekend—any extreme sport will do—and then they come back to the office on Monday morning and brag about their bruises, nicks and sprains." They also embrace tattooing and body piercing as personal expression, right along with the pain inherent in such pursuits.

Her think tank also discovered that 20-somethings define "pain" more broadly, beyond the physical infirmity Tylenol is used to addressing. They speak of broad-ranging feelings, as in broken-heartedness, spiritual emptiness or loneliness. Thus, they seek relief from pain in a variety of ways in which Tylenol simply is not equipped to compete: They go to acupuncturists, pastors, spiritual advisers, bartenders.

What's a brand to do? "The issue for Tylenol," according to Faith, "was not so much that it wanted to grow its business today with these young adults." Rather, the brand wanted to forge an emotional connection with them, a memory trace that would be there, to reawaken later, when they began to experience pain in a more traditional (read: *aging*) way.

So, Tylenol and BrainReserve embarked upon a nontraditional quest: to show up where pain was happening, not to offer an easy fix, a pill-popping solution, but to "be there" with them, to share their enthusiasm for their sports, the cause of the pain and to partner with them. They set up hospitality tents at major and minor events throughout the country, without the usual signs screaming the name of the brand, and invited top-rung, respected skateboarders like Tony Trujillo to just hang out with them between events. They funded the renovation of an indoor skateboarding bowl in Brooklyn, which was immediately and internationally dubbed by skaters as The Tylenol Bowl—again, no corporate signage attached.

The brand created an unusual set of initiatives: Ouch! Tattoos (applied with water, happily), 'zines that told painful stories, and on and on. The group created Ouch! The Web Site, with short films, short stories (*The Pleasure of Paying in Pain, Rawhide, Little Scars, Beauty Hurts*) and guides to upcoming events.

Soon, spontaneous combustion began to occur: A *Saturday Night Live* skit featured Tylenol as the antidote to extreme pain (testicular trauma, in true not-ready-for-prime-time fashion). A cartoon in the *Philadelphia Inquirer* featured "extreme sledders" (a spoof on extreme sports) calling for Tylenol. The group commissioned a filmmaker to create a short movie, an ode to nagging pain. After that, the floodgates opened, with fans of the brand submitting their own short films, story ideas, 'zine concepts, photographs and more. This was a true "breeder-reactor" moment; it welled up in the pop culture, unattended by public relations campaigns or "buzz" marketing hype.

In short, the brand bonded with this age group for the long term through cultural relevancy, by going to them, rather than through the interruption marketing of a 30-second television spot, or the quick fix of a price promotion in a college bookstore. In return Tylenol made under-the-radar headway with an important emerging group as it presumably ages into caring about pain alleviation, without having to give up Tylenol's more conventional doctor-in-a-white-coat image so well known to those of us who watch nightly national news.

The fun, the enthusiasm, the respect of the brand for its users comes screaming through: What other kind of pain medication will they ever buy? And every time they reach for it, won't it reignite those days on boards? *Shopportunity!* for decades ahead. Price, be damned.

Marketers love to think of consumers as "breeder reactors," but of course, we don't see ourselves that way. What we seek are the multidimensional excitements the best brands deliver. The most elementary promise a soft drink like Code Red can fulfill comes from its tangible attributes: It's liquid, so it can quench our thirst. Code Red and its Mountain Dew cousins all boast a fair jolt of caffeine, so it can also turbocharge our after-school experience.

Code Red and Tylenol are fascinating products not because one's a soft drink teens like, or another's a pain-reliever 20-somethings might someday use, but because each delivers a particular kind of cultural connection that is as social as it is physical.

Carrying a Code Red bottle badges its drinker as cool, an insider. An Ouch! Tattoo badges its user in the same way. The life span of that brand promise depends on how it is marketed, who buys it and what its vision is for itself—all intangibles that go well beyond what a brand actually does. This is the essence of a badge brand. We use it to telegraph the story of ourselves to others. In order to get the message through, others have to share our understanding of what our choice of Code Red, of Tylenol means. It's fair to imagine that the mothers who demanded their grocers get Code Red thought their sons liked its taste. The sons weren't talking. They just took Code Red with them and used it to convey their own hip, insider consciousness to their peer group. Mothers of kids with Ouch! Tattoos probably just heaved a sigh of relief to learn this one washes off.

Only the marketing establishes meaning here: Is one soft drink intrinsically better than another? One pain reliever? One pair of jeans? One kind of vodka? One pair of sneakers? Perhaps, but since most are pretty good, promises of product performance pale, while the product's ability to enhance our identity escalates in value. Most of the meaning of the product is in the brand and how it badges us.

What shoppers and the people who sell the products don't often understand is this power of the badge. As we have become less tethered by family ties and community, we use our brand selections to shorthand our personal DNA to ourselves, our friends and strangers.

We are human beings, social beings. When we have an experience, positive or negative, we need to speak of it. That may mean name dropping a hot new restaurant, casually mentioning we drive a Porsche, weaving into conversation the price we paid for those jeans.

Even when we're not speaking, we're still whispering through the scores of brand decisions we make every day of our lives. I don't have time to explain myself all the time to everyone, so look at my watch, my shoes, my key chain, my earrings, my bag, my briefcase, my jeans, my jacket. I'll tell you as much as I can, without saying anything. And I'll get a dose of emotional succor with it. If my choices are significant to you, then might not I be too?

We are, in essence, branding ourselves: badging. We wear the brand logo to hotwire the news of who we are.

But what if you don't want to participate in the culting of brand? What if, as a friend of mine described, when you walk into a club store you start to cry? What if the 50,000-plus items in a grocery store or 120,000 brand bits and pieces in the typical Big Box overwhelm you? What if you just want to opt out?

Well, I'm sorry, but this really isn't an option in a consumer society. It turns out we all want to belong to some club, whether we admit it or not. Our social drivers are too powerful to resist, and the rest of our cultural connections are too frayed to provide the circuitry to hold the charge. Bottega Veneta tried to sell opting out of the branding system years ago with its slogan: When Your Own Initials Are Enough. Our own initials are so rarely enough.

Besides, where would we go if we opted out of our consumer culture? What would we do, exactly? Make our own food, grow it, harvest it, consume it? Knit our own clothes? Scoop up the bacon grease and fireplace ashes to make our own soap? Revert to the life that Katherine was so eager to leave behind? No. We really cannot go back again. We may glance longingly in the rearview mirror now and again, try to make fresh bread now and again, or join a knitting circle, but there, right at the edge of our world is the inescapable wall of consumption. Precious little will be gained by hurling ourselves against it.

Seen from one angle, of course, this marketplace is depressing. Our brands slouch forward incrementally. They create progressively less rousing news. The less moving the news a product delivers by virtue of its tangible features, the more laden the marketing of the brand must become, until we reach the current postmodern apex, in which the marketing becomes the message.

Thus, you decide to drink Budweiser because you like the frogs, not because you believe there's inherent superiority in the beer. You opt for Geico insurance because you like its sense of humor, not because its coverage is better or you have a relationship with the agent.

"Marketers know about consumers, consumers know about marketers, marketers know consumers know about marketers, consumers know marketers know consumers know about marketers," is the description offered by Stephen Brown, professor of marketing at the University of Ulster, of the funhouse mirror that brands must now be reflected in.

And when the mirror stops reflecting us in ways we value, the default setting is "low price." Thus, the current enthusiasm for Pabst Blue Ribbon beer in bars in Manhattan's Lower East Side: Termed "working-class shit beer" by denizens of these haunts, the idea is to eschew any marketing halo and drink the cheapest, down-market thing you can find. But, well, that's a badge too, isn't it, as PBR becomes the cool beer of choice.

We see a new world emerging before our eyes: At the upward edge are all the $200 jeans, Burberry anythings and $8 pints of ice cream. And at the bottom, welcome to Shopping Woebegone, where all the products are okay, all the brands are available and all the prices just a little bit below average. In the middle? The vast wasteland of cavernous stores, oftentimes deserted and usually staffed by people more eager for their next break or gossiping with a colleague than helping you find no-drip candles.

The question for us is how do we retain any genuine stake in what we consume when our needs are already met and a product's promises are irrelevant? How do we find, enjoy, sustain a genuine *Shopportunity!?*

Code Red and Tylenol both show a pathway through our modern marketspace. We may know marketers want us, but we must require them to respect us too. It requires a form of conscious consumption, an intentionality on the part of both marketer and shopper.

How? We must approach our shopping list with intentionality. We must fathom our deep longing for belonging, for connectivity and admit how it truly can be sated in a consumer culture. To require our brands and the retailers that purvey them to deliver on a more profound covenant than simple product performance or buzzworthy hype, we must know ourselves.

Let's consider the joyous upside, and I mean this straightforwardly. Every day of our lives we have scores of brand decisions to make. We are free to experiment, seek variety, and shake up our self-perception, trying on new identities, accepting or rejecting them.

Do we like canned or bottled beers, or only draft? Do we choose Crest or Colgate? Starbucks? Peet's? Folgers? Do I wear Gucci or Nike or Puma or Converse sneakers? Drive a Corvette, a Scion, a Prius or a vintage Mustang? Who are we? Perhaps when we've aptly assembled the jigsawed pieces of our personal puzzle, we get a hit of centrality. We are right and plumb, knowing where we fit in the scheme of the consumer culture in which we live.

We're not wrong to want meaning from these exchanges, or even to suspect that something powerful may be found in and through our choices of our things. By defaulting to a search for a bargain, however, we're not going to enjoy the more profound delights of human society.

Still, it's easy enough to look at Code Red and say, "Oh, but that's just for adolescents." Only teens are that insecure as to need the North Face jacket, the Slvr phone, the Chuck Taylor sneakers, this moment's must-have jeans? Hmmm. Take a look with me at your most recent business dinner or night out with friends. Let's tote up our own bar bill. One drink order to our local bartender puts adult badging in sharp relief. Let's consider how the liquor industry allows us to be ourselves, unique and specific, in front of others.

Certainly, booze is a mood-altering category of the first magnitude, ready to transform us from tired, harried, road warrior into suave, sophisticated connoisseur, raconteur and, occasionally, provocateur, and from there, ever so occasionally into bleary-eyed babbler and bore.

Any alcoholic beverage can achieve this mood-altering goal. A successful brand has to get beyond its tangible irrelevance to become something of social value, to become essential, vital, cool. The epicenter of this challenge is the public bar. Don't believe me? Just think of all the people you know who order premium booze in front of people, even strangers, but buy more middle-of-the-road brands for home consumption. Johnnie Walker Black out with clients, but Dewar's at home.

If price were the big deal we think it is, then the reverse would be true: We'd buy the best stuff for home consumption, and buy lesser brands out with friends, because of the steep markup in bars and restaurants. Three Belvedere martinis at a hotel lounge pays for an entire bottle at home, yet we buy Stoli or even Smirnoff or even Popov at home and demand Kettle One or Grey Goose or Chopin out.

No, it has to be that we're searching for something beyond simple product performance here, simple social ease, easing into inebriation. The bartender at my favorite watering hole knows this through years of patient observation. "Look, there are two kinds of drinkers," he tells me, eyes twinkling. "Social, outgoing types who come in with a bunch of friends, or who make friends right here on this stool. And there are the quiet, loner types: They're alone even when they're with someone, if you know what I mean."

It's his profession to know who is walking in, when the bar-room door swings open. Is it a lone wolf seeking the wound-licking solace of a solitary drink? Or a group of revelers there to celebrate a promotion? Perhaps a couple hovering in search of a table in a quiet corner? By assessing in that instant what the patron is seeking, the barkeep—and the brands—can deliver.

One liquor company executive told me that there's only one place you're likely to try a new drink and that's from a friend's glass. In many cases, the bartender in a neighborhood joint serves as that friend, suggesting what might be good for you this particular night. Some chain restaurants take pains to offer laminated tent cards suggesting "group drinks" in pitchers and carafes on one side, with exotic mixed drinks and premium "pours" on the other.

"Say a bunch of guys come in on a Thursday night," says Will Alfieri, executive general manager of Chevy's in Battery Park. "Some nights a boss will come in with his guys and he'll just say, 'pitchers of beer, or margaritas,' and they all drink what he's drinking." Note they're sharing the same vessel, seeking an unconscious bonding, an affinity. They seek deep belonging, not to the brand, but to the man.

Paula, a seasoned waitress, describes the women who come in a little unsure of themselves, perhaps, eager for the suggestion of Chevy's fresh fruit margarita of the day: In December, it's cranberry; in summer, watermelon. "It's not that hard to push our signature drinks: They are looking for an idea."

Will decodes the "pushing of drinks" for me. "A liquor company will create a contest and award prizes. The server or bartender who sells the most of a certain drink or a brand of beer over a two-week period gets a free DVD player, that kind of thing. Some guys win every contest. They know how to use the power of suggestion to get people to order a certain drink."

Paula agrees. "It's not that hard; you can tell if they are really looking to try something new and different." However, it isn't always relevant. "This is a neighborhood place for the brokers and commodities guys," Paula tells me. "We know them, we know their drinks. We know who orders a Patron on the rocks with a wedge of lime. Or maybe a whiskey neat. They want everyone to know: They're their own guy, that's their badge. And some days, it's the guy who always orders a beer at the bar and who suddenly asks for a shot chaser. You know he's had a rough one."

The lone wolves often order with fetishistic specificity: "Belvedere martini, straight up, one olive, rocks on the side." The communication is clear: I know what I'm doing and I'm willing to pay for exactly what I want. Stand back. Vodka makers are particularly dependent on these emotional cues because there is so little difference in taste, color or strength. That we bother to designate one vodka over another is a tremendous testament to the power of branding status.

At the dinner table, too, the desire to label lingers: "Mine is a Discerning Palate," proclaims this drinker, recalling vintages, varietals and walking tours of the Scottish Highlands, real or imagined, with ease. Reviews and *Wine Spectator* scores roll easily off the tongue.

And at the end of the evening, those same folks who wandered in for a pitcher of margaritas now want a round of sweet liqueurs to sooth the transition home. Let us sit and sip a cordial in front of the fire and enjoy our good fortune.

So, while any reasonably potent alcohol will deliver the requisite "attitude adjustment" to quicken our transition from work to leisure, we persist in attributing personal meaning to each choice. This meaning is offered by the brands through their marketing. We ratify the meaning, one bar tab at a time.

To me, the liquor industry is *Shopportunity!* incarnate: Prices constantly climbing ($14 glass of Chardonnay, $18 Belvedere martini, $22 dram of port), fashion ever evolving (Green Apple martini!, Whiskey Smash! Bellini!), nuance upon nuance that caters to our sense of emerging connoisseurship (single malt scotch, Opus One, Tangueray 10). Nobody dickers with a bartender over the price of a drink. We may arrive during Happy Hour, when the beer on draft and frozen margaritas are half price, but once inside, we total the tab only when we're sure to care the least about sticker shock. And a good time is had by most.

Next, Starbucks. A great way to understand the awe-inspiring power of this transformation brand is through a technique called Deprivation Research. It focuses on people who go to Starbucks at least five times a week (that's right, *five times a week*). The researcher pays them a fair stipend to forgo their ritual for a month. Remember, it's just the ritual they give up, solely the Starbucks experience. They can still have coffee. Indeed, they can still have Starbucks coffee. They can make it at home, buy it at the office, whatever. They just cannot go into a Starbucks. Then they are interviewed each day.

The first week, the tapes show calm, happy people, all happy to have extra dollars, and thrilled that they can still have their Starbucks hit. Soon enough, however, the videotape shows anxious, upset people, trying to buy their way out of the study, in order to return to the comfort of their daily ritual.

Walking into any Starbucks anywhere is always the same and always different. There's the comfort of the signature setting, coupled with the excitement of new brews, new foods, new tunes. And always, the weird incoherence of the ordering process, which never makes palpable sense, but always seems ultimately to work out.

Ask any Starbucks' devotee their top reason for going there and they will tell you plainly: It's a social experience. Ask Howard Schultz and he'll tell you what he told me one morning: "They all say 'social experience,' but almost nobody talks to anybody once they've gotten the coffee. It's just the comfort of other people there, making the same choice they have."

And here you have the perfect illustration of the value of a total brand experience, again embracing both physical need and social desires. The Starbucks' effect has pulled an entire industry upward with it. The real cost to make a cup of coffee may be pennies, but its transformational value? Priceless, as millions of devotees attest every day around the globe.

So *Shopportunity!* Rule Four says let's acknowledge our need to transform. It's a part of life and nothing bad happens by knowing it—or letting brands help us. Maybe it's simply a mood alternation, maybe it's a life-stage transformation, maybe it's a decision to participate in a powerful cultural progression. The point is to know what you're seeking and to invest in it.

Rule #4: *Name, Frame, Claim the Transformation You Desire*

But, of course, there is another question to be dealt with: How do we go about unleashing the power inherent in our brand choices without becoming enslaved by these choices? We must develop new coping strategies, new criteria beyond simple performance or low price or borrowed status, new ways to live authentically in this "no exit" world of consumer goods and services. In short, a new paradigm must emerge. One in which we search to use brands as authentic and, indeed, winning means of personal communication. One in which we celebrate the socializing joy of shopping, the thrill of just being among others. One in which we honor the covenant of brand community—we hold familiar pleasures in common—that is made explicit in our brand choices.

I believe that it is by following our minor joys, indeed by investing in our need to experience joy in the mundane, that we begin to understand the power beyond price of great brands. They provide something, usually intangible, that allows us to communicate our selfness and our individuality, and in some cases, our values. We're not telling ourselves about ourselves. We're telling the world and thus participating in it.

Thus, *Shopportunity!* Rule Five is to badge ourselves intentionally—and have fun doing it.

Rule #5: Badge Intentionally

But hey! if it's so much fun and so rewarding to have this intentional, social, authentic, legitimate, interdependent and essentially charming experience, why do we desperately seek love from all the wrong things? Read on.

Five

Looking for Love on Aisle Two

Charlene Margaritis is the bright, articulate, engaged shopper I have been looking for. She is also the wife of my best friend, John, and the mother of two wonderful adolescent boys, Andrew and Jaime. She has agreed to take me with her this day as she negotiates her way along Route 4 in northern New Jersey. We are going shopping.

"Usually I wake up with a mission," she tells me, putting key in ignition and edging out of the garage of their suburban town house in a gated community. "Like, perhaps I need a new cashmere turtleneck, or John needs socks or the boys, the boys always need something. They are a constant source of need. But, some days, I just want to explore. I don't know what I'll find. But today, I want to find a new pair of brown leather gloves. That's our mission."

This day we go first to a mall to visit a TJ Maxx and Bed, Bath and Beyond. She wants to show me the difference. It is surely there to be seen. At each store we enter, she takes a cart, plops her purse in the top and we roll merrily along. "Just in case," she tells me, beaming at the hope of the treasures that may lurk within.

"There's never a sale at Bed, Bath and Beyond," she explains, "but they do have signs that say, 'great everyday savings.'" And they do have a helpful sales staff, able to explain the difference between 600- and 1000-thread-count sheets (higher than 600 thread-count, the fabric becomes too fragile, so high-count sheets are essentially double-ply, fortifying and extending the wear).

They also deliver in spades on the "Beyond" part of the promise: Right in the middle of the aisle between bath products and bedding is an inflatable basketball hoop and ball set for sale. Huh? A seeming 'tween is enjoying himself with a session of ersatz hoops, but in the midst of the mayhem, you wonder, "Why isn't he in school?" And then, "Oh, Look, there are the lint rollers." There are also gift boxes of industrial strength proportions of margarita mix, cosmopolitan kits (just add vodka and ice), and five-bottle "collections" of Jones Soda for $9.99.

She shows me their assortment of crystal candlesticks and points out that a pair of them, eight inches high, is $49.99. "When we go to TJ's, we'll see what we can get them for there," she tells me. "Something like these, I'd buy for a house gift, if we were going for dinner or a weekend." No gloves here, though.

Upstairs in the much messier and even more "beyond" of TJ Maxx, we find handbags sorted not by style or brand name, but by color. All the brown bags together, all the blue ones. We see coats, coats and more coats, slammed so densely together there is no way to pry them off their racks, much less try them on, crammed together with no obvious means of determining size, other than eyeballing them. We soldier on, finding the crystal: There's one nine-inch candlestick, one seven-inch, one five-inch. They seem fine, but on second inspection, the bottom half is a bit cloudy. They are $7.95 each.

"If I needed a gift," she tells me, "I might buy three of these of varying heights." But she does not need a gift today. We look at gloves. TJs has leather gloves, but they are flawed: The seams along the fingers seem to bubble a bit. If she liked them more, she'd negotiate to get a special price.

She knows this store. If she liked a pair of gloves and there were six or seven pair that were the same, she'd check the price tag on each one, because it has happened that sometimes they are mismarked. I ask her to clarify: Sometimes the same type of item is marked with different prices? By mistake? Yes, she nods. I ask her which one would she buy? The cheaper or the more expensive? She does not think I'm funny. Would she tell them about the discrepancy? No. She'd buy the one marked for less, unless there was something wrong with it, in which case she'd bring both the good and bad pair to the register and ask for the better one for the lesser amount.

We pass quickly by the dressing rooms. Would she try on something here? Yes, it's okay as these things go. Not quite Loehmann's. In fact, once she tried on a leather jacket here and another woman saw her and said, "You have to get that! It looks fabulous." And so she bought it. Charlene tells me that in lieu of good sales help, oftentimes the social connection is made between strangers in the dressing rooms.

"But you have to evaluate the evaluator," she explains. "If someone compliments me on an item, I take a quick look at them to see if I can trust their opinion. You have to look at what they're wearing and evaluate their taste. When I go shopping, I wear good clothes and makeup and my hair is as good as it's going to look all day. My mother taught me that. I want to see the clothes to best advantage, not tell myself that something would look better if I was wearing makeup or had done my hair. It helps you really see what you're getting."

We go to Appleby's for lunch. It is over fried chicken salad and French onion soup that I begin to understand something. Charlene is telling me about last night's dinner at home. She'd had dinner at Rao's in New York City with John several months before. The lemon chicken had been memorable. In a ShopRite recently she'd seen a "kit" of sorts to make Rao's lemon chicken at home, so she'd bought it. Last night, she'd created the dish for all four of them. John said, "This recipe is a keeper." Andrew had said it was "okay." Jaime refused to eat it and asked instead to order in pizza.

"It's the never-ending part of cooking dinner and cleaning up after it that is the most thankless part of all of this," she tells me. "I take the inventory, I never run out of anything, I live within a food budget and I make sure that we have all seven kinds of mustard that our family likes. But if I ate 'thank you's,' I'd be starving."

Charlene and many of us, I suspect, are looking to products and brands to help sustain relationships and to foster the give-and-take of effort and appreciation: There is an emotional content to many products, as surely as there is a nutritional one. We don't mind the effort if it's viewed as significant enough to be noticed. To gain a thank you from an adolescent boy is hard work, at best. When one product doesn't perform, we try another: Jaime likes cookies. Let's be sure to get those at Costco. Like a roulette player, we don't know on exactly which number the "thank you ball" will land, so we keep betting.

From lunch we march on, through some outlets: Saks Off-Fifth (no gloves that fit the bill) and a Gap outlet, where I succumb to the lure of a magenta winter parka with fake fur trim for Mattie ($15.95, marked down from $79.95).

We buzz through Target (many gloves, but not the right ones), where the signs are clear and bold, the "headers" on the racks efficiently proclaim the price of everything underneath, the merchandise is well-ordered and abundant and the sales help MIA. It's like one of those science fiction movies where the taser rays eliminate the people, but the buildings stand. Target is a monument to powerful design; you almost don't need anyone to help you. Still, every once in a while, it would be nice.

And now on to Costco. The difference even from the outside is apparent. The clean clear Target sign, with its bold red three-dimensional letters is princely next to the "Costco" stenciled on the wall of a warehouselike building. Everything happily screams cheap here. The carts are huge. The aisles, the towers of products, the refrigerated cases: All make the statement, "We've got lots of stuff and so it must be cheaper here."

Charlene is a big fan of Kirkland, the store brand of Costco. She tells me she first tried its liquid soap—How bad could liquid soap be? she thought—and it is excellent. From there, she tried Costco's rotisserie chicken, which has become a genuine family favorite. She won't stoop to Kirkland canned tuna, however. It's just not worth the risk, in her family, big tuna fish salad fans all around.

Charlene's list has seven items on it. We will emerge 45 minutes later with more than 20, each new acquisition chosen to elicit the elusive "thank you" from someone. One of the items is returned before we leave: Charlene is having 14 people for Thanksgiving and needs a foldaway table to augment hers. We find one, 60 inches long, that will be perfect. We wrestle it to the checkout counter; it doesn't fit in the cart, so I lurch through the store with it.

She brings the car around and, of course, it doesn't fit in the trunk or backseat. She goes back into the store to ask for help. She's given some twine and told that "Allen" will be by shortly. He is. He cannot help. Insurance regulations forbade him from being helpful, from even suggesting ways to lash the table to the car. It doesn't seem to faze him; he is not interested in one more $50 sale, or in the Thanksgiving dinner she plans. Charlene explains that she'll have to return the table. He shrugs. Back it goes. She will borrow a neighbor's van and be back tomorrow.

It does not occur to either of us at that moment that somewhere along Route 4 or on Main Street, Englewood, is a small, struggling family-owned hardware store with a $70 table they'd deliver to her, for no additional charge. Charlene will have her

Thanksgiving, she will have it on budget, and with all the family favorites arrayed and seating for 14. She will persevere mightily through the deep indifference of her local Big Box, with the help of van-owning friends and hours devoted to the task to create this archetypal feast. I hope her boys said "Thanks."

Charlene is not alone, of course, in thinking that things can convey emotion. They do, but not always perfectly. Sometimes the transmission becomes garbled, as when she makes up the Rao's chicken dinner deficit by getting Jaime the cookies. But more than the nutritional content, it's the emotional content she wants to deliver: she wants him to know she loves him.

Love, perhaps the emotion most universally desired, is the one we most often attempt to convey through things. Certainly, an engagement ring is meant to carry a great deal of personal meaning; ditto, wedding rings. They say, "love," and according to De Beers, if it's one of theirs, it says "forever." (Although no ring company has gone the extra step of issuing a guarantee, or presumably been sued for nonperformance.)

There are, of course, all kinds of love. Romantic love, friendship, family love and mother's love. And, thus, there are certain brands that become Lovemarks, the ones that provide an emotional connection with their consumers. It's a term coined by one of P&G's advertising agencies, Saatchi & Saatchi Worldwide, which it later turned into an entire book devoted to the topic.

Again P&G leads the way on the understanding of the concept of Lovemarks, which A.G. Lafley, chairman, president and chief executive officer of P&G, explains as fully delivering on the twin torture tests of brand purchase.

"The best brands consistently win two crucial moments of truth," he writes in the foreword. "The first moment occurs at the store shelf, when a consumer decides whether to buy one brand or another. The second occurs at home, when she uses the brand— and is delighted or isn't. Brands that win these moments of truth again and again earn a special place in consumers' hearts and minds; the strongest of these establish a lifelong bond with consumers."

While all brands have the capacity to consistently deliver and earn some kind of respect and trust that ultimately becomes love, I believe that mother's love is the type of love that seems, as Charlene suspects, to best be conveyed by food.

"We knew at Nabisco that sweet baked goods symbolize a 'mother's love' to generations of Americans," explains Daryl Brewster, former president of the snacks and cereal sector of Kraft Foods and now CEO of Krispy Kreme. "One way you know you're getting that love is when the product literally 'melts in your mouth.' One of our jobs is to ensure the process you encounter on the way to receiving that 'mother's love' through our products replicates that original progression as closely as possible."

When confronted by a son who didn't love the meal she'd prepared, Charlene intuitively went right to the cookie aisle at Costco to get back on track. His mother loves him.

Charlene on our *Shopportunity!* hit many of the elements that the hypnotized women had pointed us toward. *Anticipation?* Surely. She may still be looking for the perfect pair of brown leather gloves. *Pursuit?* You bet. *Prominence?* The perfect gloves matter to her and she won't settle for less than exactly what she's envisioned. *Appreciation?* I can't help but believe that once she finds them, they'll be cherished.

But she stumbled, too. And on a crucial aspect of shopping. Her quest for significance through things is determined not by her assessment of the purchase, but by someone else's, in this case, Jaime's. The way she knew she was successful was not by her own evaluation, but by the hoped for "thank you" he may or (probably) may not deliver. That puts reaching the joy of a *Shopportunity!* well outside our grasp.

Jaime didn't notice the new sheets she bought for him, and he hated last night's dinner, but he was overwhelmed by the new cell phone. Who knew? She had to try everything. How about that cookie, Jaime? The finite reality of a budget forces us to search for the best deal on the goods we're going to bet on to deliver not "the goods," but an emotional hit of love. This exerts tremendous price pressure because we're hedging our bets.

The sixth law of *Shopportunity!* must be to model Charlene's dress for shopping success edit: Refuse to wear a sweat suit and sneakers and refuse to be treated like you are wearing that garb. Adopt her "no excuses" credo: Look your best when you're in the hunt and you're more likely to have a realistic appraisal of new apparel.

Rule #6: Dress for Shopping Success

The seventh law also comes from Charlene. Become the evaluator of your own purchases: Do *you* love them? (Charlene never did tell me what *she* thought of the Rao's chicken dinner she cooked at home.) Or are you using them to communicate love to someone else? Do you *want* to do that? It's okay if you do. It's always grand to buy the breakfast cereal your husband loves even if you don't. It's a thoughtful gesture. But it requires awareness. Or else you find yourself in the bargain basement, betting on the roulette wheel of consumption in order to gain love—and losing.

Rule #7: Buy What You Love—Or Know Why Not

Let's press onward, down, down, down through the price spiral.

Six

The Cheapening of
the American Dream

Consider the lowly pickle, taken for granted, and noticed only when AWOL. Then, consider the gallon jar of Vlasic pickles that sent the brand, the company and the category spinning out of control. As documented by Charles Fishman in *Fast Company,* the saga begins with Wal*Mart's decision to price a virtual year's supply of pickles at $2.97.

"They were using it as a 'statement' item," Pat Hunn, the Vlasic executive at the front line of this bargain, told Fishman. "Wal*Mart was putting it before consumers, saying, 'This represents what Wal*Mart's about. You can buy a stinkin' gallon of pickles for $2.97. And it's the nation's number-one brand.' "

Vlasic was a respected brand with a well-earned reputation for delivering a high-quality product, worth a bit extra than store brands, marketed with a degree of Marx Brothers wit.

Then, Vlasic went bankrupt.

"The real story of Wal*Mart, the story that never gets told," according to Fishman, "is the story of the pressure the biggest retailer relentlessly applies to its suppliers in the name of bringing us 'everyday low prices.' It's the story of what that pressure does to the companies Wal*Mart does business with, to U.S. manufacturing and to the economy as a whole. That story can be found floating in a gallon jar of pickles."

The gallon jar, priced below $3, sold an estimated 80 jars a week at each of Wal*Mart's then 3,000-plus stores. That's nearly a quarter of a million gallons of pickles flooding the American kitchen, weekly. The impact was quick and quickly devastating: Why buy pickles—any kind, any size—anywhere else?

Reportedly, after a point, consumers started throwing out the remains of the jars—which, after all, did not fit in the ordinary refrigerator—because it was cheaper to buy the large industrial size and toss it when the pickles became moldy. Cheaper, yes. But this undercuts everything we hold dear about consumer respect for the brand—and the environment.

Wal*Mart's impact is not simply to grind brands that try to please them into the dust. It also seeks to claim the higher ground of "consumer friend" through its "everyday low pricing," all the while searching the globe for the cheapest, okay merchandise, regardless of how or where or by whom it is made.

We respond to their logic. Why? Because we allow ourselves one bargain at a time to lose our ability to evaluate the relative merits of a gallon of pickles at whatever price. We have become addicts, based on genuine changes of biochemistry. We no longer search for the perfect "thing." We're trolling for "the best deal." When we get it, a series of neutrons begin firing in our brains, generating a feeling, a chemical rush that cascades through the body, gland by gland. Dopamine, follow the dopamine.

•   •   •

"The seeking system is one of the most primitive systems in the brain," Helen Fisher, professor, scientist and best-selling author of four books including the breakthrough *Why We Love: The Nature and Chemistry of Romantic Love,* told me. "This is a circuit of dopamine pathways, and when this system is activated, we become highly motivated, focused, spontaneous and impulsive. People with lots of dopamine are very adaptable, creative and optimistic. They seek novelty, excitement, danger. Newness drives up dopamine. It's why retailers change the store windows. It excites us."

The law of associative memory suggests our personal neurological network is created when emotion reinforces an event, to underscore it in our long-term memory. So when we get that first bargain—and realize that we now have something, dress, scooter, shoes, cell phone, we didn't think we could afford—the joy juice of dopamine is unleashed. The bliss of the deal, of saving some amount of money, works precisely like cocaine on our seeking systems. Another term for the seeking system, Helen tells me, is the "wanting system," and what we want is a bargain, at any price.

Dopamine is also the main chemical associated with addiction. It helps confound us, getting us to want, even crave, those things we do not need. When it is released, it courses throughout our brain, seeking cells in which to dock. The more we save, the more we need to save, in order to preserve the rush. The harder we work to maintain the high, the more tightly wired we become, the more interdependently linked our receptor cells and neurotransmitting dopamine become. Like keys in a lock, only a bargain will open the portal to the rush we crave.

We find ourselves in a dilemma: Since you can't control this quest for the emotional state you're seeking, you're addicted to it. You must feed the beast. The beast tortures you with improbable promises. You can save for college while buying more stuff. You can get a five percent rebate when you use your AmEx Open card to get more stuff. You can get a special discount and private shopping hours when you buy enough stuff at Costco to qualify for Executive Status. Feed this beast you will.

The difficult truth is that the moment you purchase a product, it begins to become less valuable. The car begins to depreciate the moment you drive it off the lot. The shampoo does not give you an orgasm in the shower, it just gets used up. The toy in the cereal box breaks before the Frosted Flakes are gone.

In theological terms, it's an element of Original Sin: "Some of us love to get the newest, the latest things," says the Reverend Timothy Keller, of Redeemer Presbyterian Church in New York City. "Before and just as we get the new car, the new clothes, the new job, the new relationship—we get a feeling of exhiliration. If we are honest with ourselves, we are looking to the new things for transcendence. Everyone we love is dying. But we long for a world in which duration brings ever increasing beauty, strength, brightness, freshness."

The half-life newness with its promise to make us special, to confer its freshness upon us, decays quickly. Day by day, week by week, the car loses its luster, we forget how it smelled, how we wanted to just go for a ride, how thrilled we were to show it off, how pristinely we maintained it, lovingly polishing its chrome, massaging its leather with oils. Soon enough, crumbs invade the carpeting, juice spills on the seats, toll tickets line the glove box.

In shopper terms, it means the brand promise is most valuable when you are just on the cusp of acquiring it, when you've thought about it and decided upon it and anticipated it. Yet that is precisely when and where retailers and manufacturers have determined to convince you that the only aspect of a product worth considering is price. Just at that moment on the precipice of acquisition, of ownership, we are told that cheap is what we should value.

How can it be that on top of the diminishing importance of a product's fine promises—frogs instead of beer—we also have a tyranny of price? A colleague of mine at Procter & Gamble put it succinctly several years ago: "One generation of marketers has addicted three generations of consumers to the heroin of price promotion." And heroin it is.

Just about now, you'd be right to wonder, is this reversible? Has any product or category made it out of the death spiral? I believe that we have to look no further than the Napa and Sonoma regions of Northern California to see a compelling illustration of how to do it. Thirty years ago, American wine was thought of in terms of jugs, with brand names like Gallo Hearty Burgundy. So I went to Napa to explore the phenomenon of reversing a well-established downward price spiral. The American wine industry banded together with a clear vision that first and foremost it could create a product that could rival the French and second that it could help educate our taste. What is fascinating is that the industry understood it needed to make the case together, not as a series of disparate brands all fighting for ever thinner slices of the same pie.

Robert Mondavi is largely credited with being the mastermind behind the strategy, so I started there. Nina Weims, curator at the Mondavi Museum, explained it to me: "Robert set the standard. He never said American wines were better; he just said they belong in the company of the best wines of the world. And he never just talked about Mondavi wines. We all understood: We had to succeed together or surely we would fail separately."

Another vintner told me, "We drink each other's wines. We enjoy each other's triumphs. There's enough success to go around. One hand washes the other, but both hands wash the face." (Imagine that, for a moment, among Black Friday retailers.)

The curator of the Napa Valley Museum put it in historical

perspective. "There were three 'shots heard round the world' for our wines: First the 1976 Bicentennial Tasting in Paris, second the 1979 Baron Philip and Bob Mondavi Opus One Partnership, third the *60 Minutes* story on the 'French Paradox.' " (Remember that? The wine drinker's equivalent to *French Women Don't Get Fat,* i.e., they drink a lot of red wine and don't get heart disease.)

Opus One changed a great deal for American wines, but hand-in-glove with this spectacular and spectacularly priced wine ($100 a bottle at the winery in the early years and more now, $300-plus in a restaurant, when you can get it) came the commitment of the industry to conduct tastings in local liquor stores, educating both retailers and shoppers. They also made the concerted financial investment in advertising in magazines that published wine reviews and hired wine writers. There was and is a tremendous commitment to the education of the American palate and as discernment rises, so do prices.

"The success of Opus One was a triumph for all of us. It raised the bar and the price ceiling," the marketing director of the Hess Collection told me. "We all benefit from quality improvement. We share our advances with each other, so that the entire valley benefits."

And, of course, there must be the recognition of the potential for abuse, as well. "We have to establish the fine line between use and abuse . . . and we have to prove we honor it," said the Napa Valley Wine Museum curator. "Remember this is the country that invented Prohibition. We're not in the liquor business. We're an elegant essential of life."

Nina Weims agreed. "Robert Mondavi was the first one to understand that wine had to be put on a level playing field with art, music and gastronomy. He brought Alice Waters here. He created the Culinary Institute here. He brings great musicians. His wife inspires the museum."

It recalls a saying from the Dalai Lama: Shopping is the museum of the 20th century. Well, don't we wish. I think American wine does point a way out of the muddle we're in. It will come in the education of our taste and discernment regarding style, detail, the essential wit of good fashion, the long-term value of quality and the quiet joys of the best in class.

Paying higher prices for good wines created an entire upward movement for the industry, based on its commitment to painstaking consumer education and a belief in the consumer to respond to a superior product. It can be argued that once derided American cuisine has made the same transition from lowly stepchild of the French to genuine badge of taste, discernment and, well, sticker shock, on occasion. But clearly such gustatory pursuits are not affordable for all.

Economists Pankaj Ghemawat and Ken Mark defend the crucial role the race to the bottom plays for economically strapped shoppers. When Wal*Mart enters a market, prices decrease by 8 percent in rural areas and 5 percent in urban areas. According to these two, "Without the much maligned Wal*Mart, the rural poor, in particular, would pay several percentage points more for the food and other merchandise that after housing is their largest household expense."

This is the viewpoint that posits Wal*Mart has had more to do with holding down inflation than Alan Greenspan over the past decade. Well, maybe. Yes, consumers view wine and elegant eats as a lifestyle pleasure for which they will pay more to enjoy quality—and we should—but even in the daily drumbeat to buy our everyday food and household products, cheaper isn't always better.

A girdle may cinch in a waist to fit into a ball gown, but you mustn't look too closely at the thighs under the petticoat. The bulge must go somewhere. So too with "everyday low prices." Where is all this savings? Savings accounts? Prepaid mortgages?

More likely the spending to save this much is actually pretty well toted up in our rampaging credit card debt and soaring credit card interest rates. I know where else the bulge appears: Are we saving so very much, or are we saving on such gigantic packages of food—the 300-count cookie packages, the double packs of frozen fried chicken, the gallon jars of mayonnaise—whose only requirement is that once we bring them home, we must consume them? Are we saving on things we do not need and which, in the long run, hurt us, shorten our life spans, commit our children to lives with diabetes?

Charlene educated me, too, on another facet of "everyday low price," when she pointed out the Dyson vacuum cleaner at Target for $495. I lingered a bit too long in front of the vacuum. Charlene interrupted my reverie quickly: "Look at how shoddy the handle is," she said, gesturing at the object of my lust. "It's not at all like the real Dyson. They must make a Target version, in order to get it down to that price."

The point here isn't whether or not Dyson makes a Target version. When I go on the Internet and compare prices between the models on the Dyson Website and the ones on the Target site, they appear to be equivalent. No, the point here is the suspicion shoppers bring to the wares when we find it priced at too much of a discount. Even when we buy it, we suspect it's not quite as good. We immediately discount the joy of acquisition.

Here's another place the bulge goes: Cheap goods take a bite out of wages. Do we stop to realize that the discounter's race to the bottom enables policies such as refusing affordable health care benefits to employees, fighting against unionization or any other form of employee empowerment, looking the other way at sweatshop labor practices abroad? Do we pause to consider that by caring only about price we collude to push manufacturers to carve the very margin out of the system that would enable them to keep their manufacturing lines running while paying a living wage and investing in research and development to bring new value and innovation to the marketplace?

What happens to us when we buy on the cheap without even noticing the shoddy workmanship we're financing? What about when there are no more costs to be carved out of the system, no more corners to cut, and yet Wal*Mart pushes still further? Soon enough, product performance must be sacrificed and we begin to tumble down the rabbit hole. When the actual product no longer performs as we imagined, when the functional, basic promise is no longer delivered, what happens?

The downward price spiral moves branded, transformational badges to become mere commodities. The upward moving markets move to difference and specialness. So what is left to commodify, once we believe that all products are essentially okay, available and cheap? Well, how about workers?

I once interviewed a couple of dozen grocery store clerks, typically women, from around the country. One that stands out, I'll call Stella. She is asked to stand at a shift for eight hours a day, running products through a scanner as they come at her on the conveyor belt. The scanner enters the amounts, totals the sum, tells her what change to make. The cash register will remind her to mumble, "Have a nice day." A sign informs customers that if Stella doesn't say, "Have a nice day," they'll get a $5 coupon.

She is only an impediment, noticed only when things go wrong: We know the hazy call through the murky microphone for a price check on Register Three. We know the heavy-laden sigh when we bring out a checkbook. We know the moment when our request brings the whole enterprise to a halt because she does not know how much the decorated Christmas fire screen is, or even if it is for sale, nor do the first three people she asks.

Stella is keenly aware she embodies only the potential for human error. She travels 45 minutes each day to get to this job and 45 minutes home. Her children are in day care after school. She will hurry to get them before the facility closes, she will perhaps treasure a few moments before the sitter arrives and she goes to a bowling alley to work as a waitress in the cocktail lounge, working the eight to midnight shift. Standing, standing, always standing.

My purpose in interviewing these women was to figure out how to get them to make the customer experience more positive. We had drawn up many hypotheses. Perhaps they could be trained to dispense laundry care advice if they noticed the customer buying stain remover or bleach. Perhaps they could hand out recipe cards if they saw a patron buying green peppers and onions. Perhaps they could give children's party entertaining guidance, if they saw someone buying plastic forks, cups and a birthday cake.

The idea was that manufacturers would provide the training, the stores would authorize the time for the training, and the women would become a resource to the consumer, creating the kind of relationship that would bond shopper to store. As I sat in the break rooms with these women, or went outside to talk with them while they smoked, there was a uniform reaction. All that was all well and good, but what would really make them happier on the job, what would really make them look up and notice what the shopper was buying, what would really make their day better was one thing and one thing only: a stool to sit on.

I asked the chief executive officer of this major national supermarket chain why they couldn't have stools. He looked at me in amazement. "Do you know how many checkout lines we have? That would be a fortune."

So instead we accept the IV drip of fury that leaks into most major chain stores, whether department, grocery, mass merchant, drug, convenience or fast food restaurant. We become inured to the indifference that barely masks a seething resentment, many times a class resentment between buyers and sellers.

The workers are furious because they are being asked to perform like automatons and are pretty certain that as soon as technologically possible, they will be replaced by self-service machines. If they were bank tellers, they'd be ATMs by now. As store clerks, they are too furious to care if the restrooms are clean. They are damn sure they're not going to clean the restrooms themselves—and they prefer to tell you that restrooms aren't for customers, because who the hell cares if someone comes into the store with a three-year-old on the cusp of being potty trained? They are furious and full of a "get-a-life attitude ready to boil over," when asked where Chilean sea bass might be.

The essence of the American Dream was once able to be pretty neatly summed up in one phrase: "If you work hard in America, you have to get ahead." The right combination of hard work, courage, determination, luck and pluck enabled millions to achieve prosperity, but equally to become upwardly mobile, socially. The dream is to move out of the caste into which you were born, to forge a life that is at once far better than your parents' was and nowhere near as good as your children's will be.

For those working hard and yet not getting ahead, the culture now provides multiple pathways to *seem* to have, rather than have. So we want the home, but we use the "interest-only" mortgage to achieve it. No mortgage burning party in our neighborhood, only a usurious monthly bill with nothing to show for it after 30 years.

We can't afford good quality furniture? Well, we can have the "look" of quality, via design, without the actual expense of the workmanship that doesn't, after all, show. We can indeed have an Essential Home armoire from Kmart for $264.49, made from cardboard, plastic laminate and particleboard, boasting drawers attached by screws. It's a look, to be sure, but one that most likely won't survive a year of use.

So we aspire to and cannot quickly attain the lifestyles of the Olsen twins? We can include their $3.50 a day Starbucks habit in our student budgets. If you do the math on a $3.50 a day coffee, it's roughly $1,000 per year, over the course of a four-year college education, the loan-signing students have agreed to pay back $4,000 for an admittedly pleasant cultural prop, once they land a job.

Faith Popcorn coined the term for this trend "Small Indulgences," the practice of people who cannot afford the life to adopt signature, affordable elements of the "lifestyle." The Boston Consulting Group wrote an entire book on this phenomenon, *Trading Up,* describing the pursuit of such minor luxuries as full-fat ice cream, frappaccinos and designer pasta sauces.

But there's a dark side to these seemingly benign pursuits of small perfection. I call it "Cheat Chic," and at its zenith it is what allows us to rationalize our need for a Prada bag knockoff, turning a blind eye to its manufacturing pedigree. According to a report in *Harper's Bazaar,* "If you buy one of these fake bags, you are supporting child labor, organized crime, even terrorism." The article goes on to quote Andy Spade, CEO and creative director of Kate Spade and Jack Spade: "If women were aware that [the production of] these bags means employing illegal labor, including children, I don't think they would be having Tupperware-style parties to sell them."

I hope not. But if we're addicted to savings, then the call of a $5 Gucci handbag may trump concern about its manufacturing process: Cheat Chic.

If the essential joys of a great *Shopportunity!* like a wedding dress or first car include anticipation, pursuit, prominence and appreciation, then why are we willing to drive miles to a Big Box store, wait overnight in the cold, leaving our spouses home alone on Thanksgiving night and modeling what Christmas gift giving means to our children by pushing other shoppers out of the way when the doors finally open? If patrons waited outside for a bar to open and then rushed in, brushing others aside to get a stool, we'd have a name for them: Lush. If a junkie whining on the street corner for a fix acted this way when his supplier showed up, he'd be arrested.

Even a brief look at the totals of Black Friday 2005 shows that it is the savings addicted who are willing to sit on a lawn chair before dawn in front of the Big Box discounters. The rest of the shoppers are put off by such shenanigans and stay home in droves. And 7.4 million of us with access to computers that weekend simply went online, toting up billions of sales, basking in the glow of convenience and creating Cyber Monday.

But this begs the larger question: Why even on normal shopping days are we willing to negotiate the vast parking lot to push a huge cart through canyons of products arrayed on pallets, to be handed no boxes or bags through which to convey them, to be offered no help in schlepping them, all for the greater glory of saving money on products we didn't know we needed when the automatic doors first parted for us? Why are we willing to cheat to get the look, but not the quality, of chic? Why do we strive to buy so much for so little, comparing unit price zealously and then, when we're at last at the checkout counter, do we squander that savings on the "impulse" items at the end of every aisle and near every cash register? Are we desperate for 48 packs of Juicy Fruit? When did we first know we needed it so?

Something is happening to us. Something that involves the confusion of needs and wants: the essence of addiction. We are in the true meaning of the word "addicted" to the snake-eating-its-tail cycle of savings: In order to save, we must spend.

As Joseph Nocera wrote tellingly in the *New York Times,* "We could shut down Wal*Mart and allow small local stores to thrive by doing one simple thing: shopping at the latter instead of the former. But we don't do that . . . and for the simplest of reasons: Americans love a bargain."

The closing line of his piece asks the question, "Do we really want to change Wal*Mart?" And I would add, and the culture of okay, available and cheap? His answer, of course, is tough medicine: "We need to change ourselves first."

A great way to check our impulse to buy now is the method a friend of mine uses when confronted with a sale: Would I buy this at the regular price? It's just a great litmus test. If "yes," proceed with caution; if "no," walk away.

So, get in charge of your dopamine. Rule #8 is kick your addiction to price. How? Stop discussing the price of anything you buy. Don't mention it, high or low. Find something else to discuss about a new purchase. Delve into the details beyond the deal. And notice if this is hard for you to do. If it is, you're addicted. Find the joy in the product, not the price.

Rule #8: Kick Your Addiction to Price

Rule #9 on our way to *Shopportunity!* Don't compromise on the everyday. Differentiate between the brands you need (must have) and the brands you want (nice to have). Educate yourself on the must haves in order to buy "best in class" of your legitimate needs (and this means toothpaste, toilet tissue and turkey wings, too). Then, learn to defer and anticipate your wants until they either become authentic needs or you forget about them.

Buying better can actually reduce the amount you spend in total, because each thing is worth noticing, worth its weight in consciousness. Monitor your spending for a while. If we all begin to pay a tiny bit more—or buy fewer but better things—we can return dignity to the shopping experience and ensure that the people who wait on us are paid a living wage.

No more mindless, rote purchases—or eating. Buy what you

need for the week, from people you respect and who respect you and their wares. It will move shopping off the chore list and into Adventureland.

Rule #9: Don't Compromise on the Everyday

Rule #10: Look the clerks in the eye. Ask *them* if they're having a nice day. Try to engage in some way. If they won't, can't, don't respond, then shop somewhere else, but give it a try.

Rule #10: Look Clerks in the Eye and Ask about Their Day

Now, armed with these first ten rules, we move on to explore each *Shopportunity!* available to us in the beginning of the 21st century. From department, specialty, grocery, club and convenience stores, right up to automotive, infomercials and online— let's go behind the counter, see what's working and why, and what's not. Let's go shopping.

Section Two: The Siren Call of the Transaction

Seven

Department Stores and
How They Blew It

Now it is Cheryl's turn. Her eyes are as heavy as Hal has commanded: She is in that hypnosis state where day recedes and yesterday or ten years ago looms large.

"My husband and I go every year to Las Vegas. It's part of his job," she says, mumbling a bit.

"Speak louder," Hal suggests. "I need to hear you."

She dutifully repeats, much more clearly this time. "My husband and I go to Las Vegas every year. It's part of his job."

"And why does this trip make you think about shopping?" Hal asks.

"Because there's always a very important, very glamorous cocktail party each year," she says, as if this were self-evident.

"Where's the shopping?" Hal asks evenly.

"For the dress. I need a great dress each year, something new and wonderful. It's so important to him that I look great. This past year was so, so difficult. Finding the dress."

"Tell me about that," Hal says.

"I went everywhere. I went to Prada and Gucci and just everywhere. All the boutiques. I went to a dress shop that I've always been able to rely on. Nothing."

"What happened?" he says, like a caring physician might coax symptoms from a shy patient.

"I was talking to my mother," she says. "On the telephone. I was worried. It was getting close to the date and I had nothing and I'd exhausted all my usual places to find this perfect dress. It was important and I was worried. She said, 'Have you tried Macy's?' And I laughed and said, 'Macy's!' "

"Why?" Hal plays the innocent. "Why is Macy's such an outlandish suggestion?"

"Because it's all about those sales," she tells him. "All those ads with the coupons and they sell housewares and furniture! How could they have my dress?"

"So what did you do?" he asks.

"I was desperate," she tells him. "I said, 'Mom, you have to come with me. I can't go through all that alone.' "

"And she came with you?"

"Yes. We went right up to better dresses and I was shocked. They had lovely dressing rooms, carpeted, with those three mirrors that let you see every side of you," she tells him. "Once the saleslady understood what I was looking for, she told us just to sit in the room and she'd bring us the dresses. My mother and I sat there and we talked and evaluated each dress. There were major designer names. And the saleslady understood, she really did, she got it, what I was looking for."

"Did she find it for you?" Hal asks.

"Yes! She did. It was perfect!" Cheryl seems to positively beam from the memory. "It was Anna Sui! Who would have ever thought that Anna Sui would be at Macy's! There was a great Calvin Klein too. It was almost hard to choose. I was so happy. And I needed shoes, stockings, a new bag: All of it. And the saleslady told me just to sit there and she'd go around the floor and even to other parts of the store and get the perfect things. She brought us tea in china cups and we sat there and sure enough, she had the eye! She brought four or so bags and just a couple of pairs of shoes, but each one was spot-on. I just had to choose which one I felt was more me."

"That sounds wonderful," admits Hal. He seems ready to move on. The other women in the room seem envious, almost. Feet are shuffling. Heads are shaking.

"It was," Cheryl says. "Right up until the end."

"What happened?" Hal asks, shocked.

"When it was time to pay for it, I gave her my charge card and I was getting dressed," Cheryl tells him. "And she brought the bill for me to sign into the dressing room. It was for much less than what I'd thought. Much, much less. She told me everything was 40 percent off that day, and she didn't think I was the kind of shopper who had a coupon, so she'd gone ahead and clipped one for me from the circular."

"How did that make you feel?" says Hal, like a good shrink.

"Cheap. I didn't want it to be cheap. I didn't want her to have clipped a coupon for me and I didn't like it. I thought, 'She's cheated herself out of part of her commission to do this,' and then I thought, 'maybe she thought I couldn't afford it.' I didn't like this part at all. I bought everything, but it changed how I felt about the dress."

"Did it change how you feel about Macy's?" asks Hal.

"Wait! Wait!" she says, laughing a bit. "I just remembered. And then, and then, she asks me if I want to get a Macy's card. I could get another percentage off on all this stuff." The other women laugh, too, nodding.

"So, how do you feel about Macy's?" asks Hal.

"Pretty much the way I did before," she says with a sigh. "It's for sales. I guess I'd go back if I were desperate enough, but it just kind of ruined it for me."

Voilà! The Un-*Shopportunity!*: Macy's gave up hundreds of dollars in this one sale. If the saleslady was on commission, she gave up quite a bit too, along with a smidgen of personal ethics: Cheryl did not have the requisite coupon, but the saleslady pretended she did. And what did they get in return? A slightly miffed customer in a denigrated piece of nearly fabulous Anna Sui at a, therefore, compromised cocktail party.

This experience was poised to become a great *Shopportunity!* Cheryl came to it with great *anticipation,* of course. The *pursuit* had been going on for a month before she and her mother ever entered the Macy's dressing room. The search for the perfect dress had a great deal of *prominence* attached. And certainly, the dress had the potential of *appreciating* over time.

Macy's, in the guise of its wise guide, the saleslady, seemed ready to deliver on the experience that a really great department store seems nearly uniquely well-equipped to handle. It was very nearly a wedding gown moment. Everything Cheryl needed was there under one roof, swirling around her with the saleswoman bringing it to ground. Had she wanted, Cheryl could have had a makeover at the cosmetics counter, been presented with an impressive array of new and antique necklaces or perhaps a new watch to further enhance her emerging look—and bought an espresso machine on a pure whim. It is all there.

Instead, Macy's attempted to beat Wal*Mart at its everyday low price game. There are so many *Shopportunities!* to be had under this one roof, and yet, and yet, again and again the default setting is price. Shop with me, the store begs us and tries, essentially, to bribe us. It would not have to do this. It could triumph easily over Wal*Mart and its ilk in so many dimensions that it is just sad to watch this "giving away the store" by the store.

This is not just an apocryphal tale or isolated instance. And it is certainly not just Macy's. It happened to me not a month later. My daughter and I were in Florida visiting my mother, who was recuperating from a serious illness. She was at last home and at last ready to care about what she was wearing. She wanted a certain kind of housedress that either buttoned or zipped up the front.

Mattie and I went to the Belk's in a nearby shopping center. The department store setting seemed far less confusing than to try to negotiate through all the specialty retailers. I couldn't quite see taking my five-year-old into a Victoria's Secret to figure out if they carried anything remotely appropriate for my mother after all. The moment was emotional for us: HappySad, as Mattie says. Happy that Grammy is beginning to care about her appearance and we can do something to help. Sad that it's been such a long, hard road back for her. Both my daughter and I wanted to get Grammy exactly the dresses she wanted and lots of them.

We found the housedresses, in her size, in the muted patterns and prints she would like, with zips or buttons right where she wanted them. We picked out five. We were pleased with ourselves, I have to say, congratulating each other on the wisdom and taste of our selections.

Then, the saleslady told us that everything that day was 30 percent off. Well, okay. Let's pause the replay here. Why, you may ask, is this so terrible? Well, because it was so unnecessary. Belk's gained nothing from the 30 percent it gave me.

The saleslady's name was Linda. She was a part-time worker with no allegiance to Belk's, which hires her for just enough hours to help Belk's, but not enough to require benefits be paid her. She volunteered that she was living the cash-strapped life of a retiree whose pension and Social Security aren't going as far as planned. Her husband was working part time at the nearby Ace Hardware. She was charmed by my daughter. She wanted to do something nice for us, but lacked the skill set to provide a real service. At exactly this moment, she might have said, "Some of these are zipped up the front and some are buttoned. Would you prefer having all zips or all buttons? We have an even larger selection over here," and waltzed us over to a section we missed. But no.

Instead she asked me what I thought was an odd question, "Would you like to give one dollar to breast cancer research today?" But, hey! Okay. That's a way of giving back some of the 30 percent she just gave me, right? So I said yes, of course. Then she beamed at me and said, "That's great, because now I can give you an extra 15 percent off on all your purchases."

Just why or how that happened was inscrutable to me. There seemed to be some sort of weird promotion going on, but I had the feeling that if I asked too many questions, they'd end up paying me to take the stuff home to my mother. It was bizarre. And then, of course, came the question, "Would you like to open a Belk's charge account? There's another 15 percent off of all your purchases."

We were now at 45 percent off and she was offering me another 15 percent. And again, needlessly so. How will they ever stay in business? I refused, of course, feeling obligated to explain that we didn't live near a Belk's, not that I was worried for the future of retailing. I would have happily bought the housedresses for my mother at full price. Indeed, when I took them to the saleslady I thought I was buying them at the price listed. I would have given to breast cancer research too. What is going on?

Department stores were a 19th-century innovation, most probably introduced by Au Bon Marché in Paris. They offered everything from "swaddling clothes to grave cloths" by one account. They offered standard pricing, everything marked clearly and nonnegotiable. They offered service and a willingness to let the customer wander around the store without requiring them to buy anything. This is a prime distinction. It is fair to say that department stores invented modern shopping. Patrons entered these magnificent stores with questions, not answers. They came to discover, not to place orders.

A general store, such as the one Katherine relied upon, offered wet goods (rum and such) and dry goods (cloth, sewing and knitting paraphernalia, and other essentials of the homesteader life). The proprietor would have taken her list from her when she entered, assembled the goods, added the cost to her account and either handed them to her or delivered them. She was not expected to enter unless she wanted to buy. Department stores taught her to shop, to dream, to wonder as she wandered through. The salespeople needed to be more than order takers, they needed to provide knowledge, advice, guidance, even wisdom.

That does seem to be a compelling promise: fair pricing, radical choice, professional service. The pricing piece has always been an element of department store economics. The general store took a chance with every farmer to whom it granted an account. The shopkeeper held the account in the "Receivable" category until the farmer got the cash each harvest to settle his tab. So it priced all its products at a steep margin in order to amortize the cost of bad debt.

Department stores, on the other hand, were "cash and carry" (or at least cash and delivery). They were able to pay their vendors quickly. And they were buying in much larger quantities. Thus they routinely received discounts, which were not passed along to the shopper, but which, in fact, constituted the bulk of their profit margins.

These massive, legendary department stores grew up in this country after the Civil War because of five cultural factors. First, the urbanization of the country, resulting in hundreds of thousands of potential customers within a few square miles. Second, the increasing affluence of the industrializing population. Third, the development of mass production techniques to create the affordable goods. Fourth, the revolution in infrastructure, including the architectural, building material and public transportation that allowed for "skyscraper stores," as well as the electricity that enabled late store hours, elevators and escalators. And, fifth, of course, an affordable, reliable, trainable workforce: women willing to work outside the home.

These were female arenas, to be sure. Edward Filene, who founded the Boston department store, called it "an Adamless Eden." One writer described the typical store of 1910 keenly. "Buying and selling, serving and being served—women. On every floor, in every aisle, at every counter, women. Behind most of the counters on every floor—women. At every cashier's desk, at the wrappers' desks, running back and forth with parcels and change, short-skirted women. Filling the aisles, passing and repassing, a constantly arriving and departing throng of shoppers, women. Simply a moving, seeking, hurrying mass of femininity, in the midst of which the occasional man shopper, man clerk and man supervisor, looks lost and out of place."

These saleswomen provided a challenge to the famous merchants of the day: Macy's, Wannamaker, Marshall Field. The women willing to be, in the English term, "shopgirls," were often one or two rungs lower in the economic and social pecking order of the day than the women they were to advise. An upper-class woman torn between two types of gloves, or hat, or frock for an occasion needed to respect the lower-class woman who was counseling her.

On the one hand, that meant training these women to become trusted and knowledgeable advocates for the store's wares. They gained intense preparation, deep but not necessarily broad: A millinery saleswoman would know every manner of nuance about the meaning of ornamentation on the hats, the various methods of affixing them to the head, when and where they were absolutely required, the latest in styles from Paris, without necessarily knowing much about skirt lengths or purses. They were expert in what they sold—and they knew what they didn't know. They knew how to pass the patron on to the next department.

Overall, their role was beyond mere servitude. They were to seek and find the very best solutions to wants and needs that might have been as remote as, well, the purchase of a Porsche 911 is from the mechanic who maintains it. Yes, of course, they were to nod willingly and dispatch a horse and carriage to deliver home the spool of thread the customer wanted, but could not bear to carry. But they were also to gently, firmly persuade the less than knowledgeable customer to select the dress, the curtains, the armoire, the jewelry, the shawl, the slippers, the private necessities appropriate to her station, if not what she thought she wanted at the moment.

On the other hand, it meant paying the salesladies, as they began to prefer to be called, a living wage and, in some cases such as Macy's, providing them affordable housing via company-owned dormitories. It meant, as well, promoting them within the ranks of an organization. It required the creation of a class of professionals, at once credible, authoritative and personable.

Oh, what it must have felt like to walk into one of these grand buildings. Your shoulders lower. Your heart races. Whatever you need is in here and seasoned staff will help you find it. As early as 1870 one visitor totaled up the virtual army it takes to do this right: One general superintendent; 19 assistants, each the head of a department; nine cashiers; 25 bookkeepers to track the day's sales; 30 ushers guiding shoppers to the appropriate department; 200 cash boys running to and fro with payment and change; 470 clerks serving the shoppers; 50 porters carting the heavy objects, and 900 seamstresses, plus another 500 people employed in various capacities. B. Altman reportedly had 500 pairs of horses hitched to delivery carts at the ready to travel, in order to serve customers as far as 500 miles away.

Letitia Baldrige, the doyenne of American social etiquette and

White House social secretary to Jackie Kennedy, reminisced about those stores in an article she wrote for the Op-Ed page of the *New York Times,* in 2005. "The salespeople never forgot you. They made little notes on you, your family and where you were in life each time you stopped to buy or to custom order their merchandise. It was such a safe, predictable world. It was also intensely personal—everything directed at you and no one else. . . .

"You couldn't stump a salesperson. A gift for a little boy making his first Communion? Whatever would I get for a girl being bat mitzvahed? What could I possible give a bride and groom who have absolutely everything—times 24 of them? There was always something those fabulously trained salespeople could find that no one else would have thought of—or would have taken the trouble to think of."

That personal connection, that creativity, that care seems so foreign to us now. Perhaps it doesn't seem so very crucial, so wildly important that we have that personal guidance. We have gift registries now, after all, to ensure we give exactly what the bride and groom or bat mitzvah girl desires. But that's not shopping, after all. That's order taking. Shopping must deliver on a far more significant challenge.

As Lillian Gilbreth, a woman executive in retailing, put it in a speech in 1927, "The customer must not only like the goods she has bought, the surroundings in which she has done the buying, and the people from whom she has done the buying, *but she must like herself better at the end of the transaction.*" Here we have *Shopportunity!* beautifully stated as a simple formula being systematically ignored by our retailers on a daily basis.

Why? In this era of computerized anything and everything, couldn't our purchase patterns and behaviors be analyzed to allow a saleswoman to call or email us with the news that a suit with the same kind of styling we like has just come in? That a new blouse has arrived that would refreshen the skirt we bought last season?

Surely such information is being tracked. Why are the only messages I get from retailers about deals: Free shipping, 15 percent off for opening a charge account, 30 percent off today only?

Of course shoppers today are not clones of their 19th- and early-20th-century counterparts. We are time- as well as money-starved. We have hundreds, if not thousands, more options to churn through, blasted by marketing messages up to 3,000 times per day. But doesn't that just suggest how much more crucial it is today than 100 years ago to have a store, and a salesperson within that store, use a finely focused editorial eye to help us winnow our personal wheat from the world's commoditized chaff?

A colleague of mine, Cynthia McVay, a retail consultant, told me about a study she'd done for a specialty retailer. "We analyzed more than 150 million transactions, looking for ways to segment shoppers and correlations among departments. Not surprisingly, we found that there were a handful of customers that really mattered, and that they had predictable shopping behaviors. For example, if they visited the estate jewelry department on the ground floor, it made a lot of sense to lead them by the hand to the fur department or designer clothing. As a result of the work, the store developed a very targeted personal shopper program around this segmentation, focused on servicing—and harvesting—their loyalists."

This kind of talk, of course, strikes terror in the heart of a shopper. I, for example, don't particularly want to be harvested. But that's a question of semantics. The fact of such a study suggests a critical fault line in how these large conglomerates are run. Of course, the goal is increasing sales, and escorting a customer from one area of the store to another is a fine way to do it. But is it really necessary to analyze 150 million transactions to figure that out?

One store executive reminisced about her favorite shopping memories from a decade or more ago. She was in Bloomingdale's and she'd just bought a pair of expensive shoes. Suddenly, the shoe salesman turned to her and said, "Say, you might like a bag to go with these and my friend is in the better-bag department right now. I'll take you up there and introduce you. I'm sure he'll find something grand for you." And off they went: the shopper in the hands of a professional, not a zombie.

Nordstrom, a retailer I worked with at one point, works hard to train its salespeople as professionals and the proof is in the shopping. A great friend of mine, Bonnie Predd, chief marketing officer of an energy company, lives in Evansville, Indiana, and makes the pilgrimage to Indianapolis twice a year, just to visit Nordstrom.

"I go right to the shoe salon and I know I'll find what I'm looking for," she tells me, smiling at the memory. "The best part is when I show the salesman the shoe that I want and every time, he comes back with several pairs. Yes, of course, the one I'd asked for, but always, always another pair, nothing at all like what I'd requested. Every time, I just relax and let him sell me two pairs. I end up loving what he's brought, more than what I'd found on my own. But a great salesperson is just wonderfully relaxing. Even if they don't have my size in stock, he calmly tells me they have it somewhere in the system and it will be delivered to my home by Tuesday. Never a worry."

This kind of salesmanship takes training and training takes time, money and wisdom. How do you help a novice shoe salesman discern what second pair will meet with approval? How do you coach him or her to make an out-of-stock item seem like no problem at all, and sell through the issue to provide the inevitability of a Tuesday arrival? It is so very much simpler to offer sales and discount the merchandise than to reach out to me as an individual and say, "Hey! I think you'd like this." It's much easier to discount than to train a sales force to share sales, to teach a commissioned novice that there's a good reason to escort a shopper from one section to another. It's easier to take your best salespeople off the floor and make them "personal shoppers" in order to "service and harvest" a best customer than it is to imagine and treat every customer as potentially important.

And it's much easier to teach me that price is the issue. Why bother to educate the salesperson and through them, me, about the value of cut buttonholes? Why train her to show me to leave one unbuttoned on the suit sleeve, explaining its ability to signal the initiated that these are real, functioning buttonholes, not just pointless abstractions turned into mindless decoration?

The typical new salesperson selling coats today in a department store is paid a 6 percent straight commission (no salary) on whatever she sells, against a "draw." The draw is essentially an advance on future earnings, which ensures she can pay her bills while she's developing her skills and clientele. That means in order to make $30,000, she must sell $500,000 worth of goods. And nobody does that in year one, so she ends up technically "in debt" to the store after a year on the job. After 15 to 20 years in the business, she may hope to sell $1 million, and so maybe take home $60,000 or $70,000 a year.

The markers of quality are conveyed through a secret, silent language that must be learned. But who will teach it? Our salespeople don't have the time or perhaps the knowledge to educate us to the intricacies of excellence. Our fashion magazines don't teach, they simply badge who is wearing what designer, but not why the design is great.

In my own case the wisdom was hard-won, but deeply appreciated. Three moments of epiphany come immediately to mind. First, a particularly harsh instance when I showed up for a business meeting wearing a pair of blue gabardine pants, a fuchsia silk shirt and a bright yellow leather blazer, nude hose and brown leather down-at-heel flats. Faith Popcorn motioned me into an empty office and urgently whispered the basic rules of wardrobe:

two colors only, one of which was to be black, black or blue opaque stockings, good shoes in great condition. End of lesson. I still shiver at the memory—not for the lecture, but for its cause. It really was a garish wardrobe moment.

The second and far more calming was the balm of an experienced saleswoman on the third-floor Armani boutique at Bergdorf Goodman, trailed by her pin-cushion-at-the-ready alteration lady. I remember well the relief of two panic-stricken Thursday nights when I came in desperate and left each time with a perfectly fitted and accessorized suit, confident for a dinner party one night and ready for a major presentation another day. I still have the suits, which are just as perfect now. They have indeed appreciated over time.

Third, Judi Roaman at her shop in East Hampton took me under her wing, ensconcing me in a dressing room and bringing me suits for work, casual clothes for weekends and teaching me by her imperial and no-nonsense demeanor to eschew jeans for all but the most casual occasions. Like gardening. She also gave me a terrific tip on how to upgrade the look of any pantsuit to Armani-esque élan: Tell the dry cleaner not to put creases in the pants, or steam them out yourself.

But I'm interested in how to discern the differences in quality and design, beyond simply the badge of brand, the assumptions of price or the mentoring of friends and colleagues. I turn to Diane Podrasky, the mother of one of Mattie's schoolmates, and vice president of women's sales at coat designer Andrew Marc. Are all coats the same, but some chains simply have better buyers, able to negotiate better deals on behalf of their shoppers?

"Of course, the coats you get at an outlet or a discounter aren't the same as what we make for Neiman Marcus or Saks," Diane tells me, laughing. "There is a huge quality trade-off, but many shoppers don't notice the details. Some shoppers conceive style and even quality, in general terms—a rough approximation of this year's look. We try to train the sales associates in the stores, but it's painful to admit they don't know either. And, of course, in the discount or mass stores, there aren't any salespeople to train."

At her company, the Andrew Marc Collection stands for high-end, beautifully designed leathers and wool, with fur accents, including mink, shearling and silver fox. They augment the finest, most supple English domestic leather with gorgeous fur pelts and trendy styling. The fur, back in fashion just now, is "long and luxy," in Diane's parlance: thick, able to handle dyes, boasting the variegated markings that run down the back of the animals, in contrast to the thin coats on their underbelly or the gray cast to their tails. Andrew Marc's prime prospect is a size six who shops in Neiman Marcus or Saks Fifth Avenue. The coats retail for $600 to $1,200, with shearlings going for as much as $3,000. It is this quality garment that Bergdorf Goodman would put its own label on.

The next rung down is "MarcNY, by Andrew Marc." The trade-off begins: less expensive skins, probably from China or Korea; the styling is more mainstream; the fur is rabbit or raccoon in thin strips for cuffs and collars. And, oh yes, it's cut fuller, for sizes 10 to 14. This is the "volume" label, sold to "middle tier" department stores, such as Macy's, Marshall Field, Nordstrom and Bloomingdale's. Some of these coats are "revised" using last year's trims and sold this year to Saks Off-Fifth, Nordstrom's Rack, even MarMaxx, the parent of TJ Maxx and Marshall's. You may think you're getting overstocks, but your need to believe you're getting a deal has been well anticipated. Ah! You thought, as I did that these stores sold overstocks or merchandise that didn't move at the main stores? Think again. Clothing companies make cheaper designs to look like closeouts. In this realm, they are called "in-season special make-ups." Oftentimes, there's a sign on top of the rack with an asterisk saying that the manufacturer's retail price was suggested by the manufacturer and, indeed, the clothing may never actually have been sold to anyone at that price.

Every once in a while, just to keep us going, there's an honest bargain to be found here. These stores, Neiman Marcus Last Call and others, like Loehmann's, Filene's Basement, Syms and Century 21, can also be a dumping ground for a glut of inventory, if the manufacturer gets stuck with too much of an item that isn't moving. Perhaps as much as 10 percent of a designer's wares will ultimately end up here, with the shoppers who win this lottery gaining the bragging rights, albeit to merchandise nobody else wanted.

And then comes the third rung: Private label for mass merchants, like J.C. Penney. Why? Andrew Marc makes coats for this channel, as well, with cheaper nylon and no fur, but here the designer does not sign his work. The main requirement is "big, cheap, now," one manufacturer told me, with a request for anonymity. It's important, I think, to dwell on that reality. The shoppers in these stores are considered to be impatient, tone deaf to quality and, well, big: 14 to 20. The implication is clear. These are the same shoppers who are buying the 300-count cookie packages, industrial-size peanut butter tubs and gallon jars of pickles. Addicted to the heroin of price promotion, they spend to save. They are eating their way through cookies, potato chips, and Twizzlers and into size 18 coats and extra-extra large sweaters.

Why do these merchants go to Andrew Marc, rather than deal directly with the factories in China themselves? Here, the designer brings something to the picture: trickle-down elements of design, a vision of what the private label could become, an understanding of the trends that drive fashion. Intangibles to be sure, but enough of an imprimatur to keep the merchants from going it alone, for now.

And, finally, the fourth level of the inferno: Express and other lower tier yet trend-driven, fast fashion retailers. Andrew Marc can't really be making much on $99 coats, right? Well, Diane explained it to me. The volume, maybe 20,000 coats, for each retailer, allows Andrew Marc to keep its factories motivated to do the best work for the designer line. Companies use these orders to keep the factory lines running in China. Then, when they need a high priority attached to the designer line, they command the attention of factories that are working on their goods one day and someone else's the next.

The grim news here is that manufacturers stoop to make products they don't respect, to come in on the cheap at a price point retailers demand of them. They become makers of goods they would not wear themselves, offered in a slapdash environment with no salesperson in sight. Is this race to the bottom unstoppable now?

Watch Saks Fifth Avenue, Diane tells me. "They are trying to reverse the process. They take our best coats and they are trying to work with the salespeople to really present this kind of merchandise so that the shopper can tell the difference. How else can everyone make enough money to stay in business and give the shopper a terrific experience in the store? A store like Saks cannot compete on everyday low price; it has to educate the shopper that workmanship, craftsmanship, style and details matter. Great clothing contributes a great value to our lives; it's something worth paying for."

Some manufacturers figure out a way to deliver that great value at different price points by developing brands for different price levels and then creating their own stores. I'm thinking of Armani, with its high-end couture, its ready-to-wear suits sold for $3,000 to $5,000 at Bergdorf's and Barneys, as well as Armani shops, its Emporio Armani for more casual ensembles and finally its Armani Exchange for jeans and street chic. Donna Karan has done it too, with her signature line and then the wildly popular DKNY. Tommy Hilfiger has sought to move up the price tier with his H line. Ralph Lauren loses money reportedly on every Purple Label $5,000 suit he sells, but creates a halo that covers a multitude of other Lauren products that deliver some piece of the Purple Label promise of perfection.

Each of these initiatives are moves that shift the center of retail gravity away from department stores and into the manufacturer's own stores, where they control the ambience, the merchandising, the training of the salespeople and, of course, the pricing. Simultaneously, retailers, of course, with their private label brands, seek to further blur the unique expertise each player brings to the shopping equation. When retailers make clothes and clothing designers open retail shops, what is going on? Simple. They are each trying to preserve their margins at the expense of the other.

But I was still fixated on Cheryl's experience searching for the perfect cocktail party dress at Macy's, as she'd reported it to us under hypnosis: the frenzy to price cut, even after the sale had been made. I spoke with one senior executive at Federated, which owns Macy's, Bloomingdale's, and now Lord & Taylor and Marshall Field's, among others.

"We absolutely don't believe in defaulting to low price," she assured me. "What you're describing is something we're taking real pains to work out of the system. One of the ways we believe we can protect ourselves from major brands beginning to drift toward the mass and discount chains is to create our own labels."

Hmmm. She seems earnest, but I'm not convinced. Diane has just told me about those store labels. They are pretty much the same merchandise as other stores request, just labeled differently. Because it's the store's label, the store's margin is a bit better, but how does that help the shopper? Does Federated work with the salesperson to be able to explain the subtle differences that would allow it to claim these are superior to what the shopper can find elsewhere? Are there any differences?

"Absolutely," she tells me. "I'll send you our training video, so you can see for yourself." They've started a certification program for their sales associates to learn the art and science of hand selling clothing.

Hmmm, again. Diane has told me, too, about the training Andrew Marc and most every other vendor provides the retailer. "You get there in the morning and you want to make it an event, but the salespeople aren't being paid, of course, to attend. This is on their own time. They look at me, look through me, look around me to see if I've brought breakfast. It's difficult to really make your case."

Other manufacturers have told me that they've become so disturbed by the low level of sales assistance in important "doors," as the Macy's, Bloomingdale's, and Neiman-Marcuses of the world are called, that they routinely subsidize a partial salary to a store's commissioned salesperson just to get them to focus on their product. Indeed, some high-end clothing companies are borrowing from the playbooks of the major cosmetics firms and putting their own staff in-store on a permanent basis.

My Federated confidant tells me, "Our average customer is not like our average sales associate. Most of our customers view themselves as building a career." I think of Linda at Belk's in Florida. Why couldn't she build a second career, there? Wouldn't she have had a different point of view if she did? And, oh by the way, how do you professionalize a job without having a career path? How do you learn a profession on 6 percent commission and no salary?

Sure enough the training video and sales materials arrive. Along with a PowerPoint presentation, the leader's guide and participant guide, there's a corporate fact book and two ecstatic issues of *Coast to Coast,* Federated's in-house glossy magazine. The tone of all the materials is unrelentingly chipper, as if American retail were not in fact in a free fall.

The video begins. It is about how to engage the shopper even as she looks you in the eye and says, "I'm just looking for ideas." And how to ensure that she tells you easily that she's gotten a new job, moved here from Toronto, has closets filled with business suits, but is now moving into a business-casual environment, which will nonetheless require her to travel 50 percent of the time. With that information in hand, you're ready to ensconce her in a fitting room, shop for her, and, when she pauses before buying absolutely everything you've suggested, explain to her rationally that the pants she's thinking of deferring are machine washable, so she'll save on dry cleaning bills, and that if she doesn't have a Macy's card (she doesn't), she can open one now and get 15 percent off on all her purchases for the next two days.

Augh. What's with the credit cards? Enough already.

Watching the companion *She is . . .* video, I'm struck with how the store executives are sharing this with their salespeople— as if these salespeople did not know what a shopper looked like.

"She is a real shopper," the really pleasant female voice intones and goes on to explain that this hypothetical shopper shops 78 times a year, wears casual clothes at work, is most probably married, with children. She spends $5,000 a year on her home and clothing and is proud of both. Macy's gets about 19 percent of her business now, but there's great potential, roughly $9 billion in play, to get her to come to the store more often and to gain more of her money each time she does.

They go on to describe four types of women that the salespeople should watch for. There's Katherine, the traditional shopper, who is conservative, neat and puts a great deal of effort into holiday celebrations for her family. There's Julie, the neotraditionalist, who likes classic looks, but will go for trendy sometimes, seeking convenience and comfort. Consider, too, Erin, the contemporary woman, for whom individuality is key, and who loves technology as much as fashion, sports as much as spas. Finally, there's Alex, the fashion seeker, who is dedicated to the latest, newest, greatest, and will seek whatever is hip, dropping what's not.

Cut into the descriptions, and the fast-cut video montage of how we are to imagine these women's lives, are real women being interviewed in a focus group setting. And they are real women, not the glamorous ciphers—Katherine! Julie! Erin! Alex!—who might well be a recruiting video for a road show version of *Desperate Housewives*.

Now then, what are the salespeople meant to do with this? From watching the video twice, I can only intuit they're meant to be reassured that their bosses know stuff. Weird stuff, to be sure, but stuff that seems like the kind of stuff bosses are supposed to be thinking about. And, if I were them, I'd be eyeing the tables to see if the Danish, juice and coffee had arrived.

Note to store executives: Listen to the salespeople. Focus group *them*. Pigeon band the successful ones. They have millions of interactions with shoppers every week. Stop trying so hard to "segment" consumers in an effort to what? To "harvest" the ones that "matter"? Encourage, don't avoid or eradicate, the very messy reality of individuality.

I turned next to Peter Connolly, former president of marketing for Tommy Hilfiger for many years. He started out at Macy's early in his career, went on to make Ikea a pop culture phenomenon and then Ralph Lauren, before going to Tommy. "What about Macy's?" I'd asked.

"Forget about Macy's," he told me. "They had it and they threw it away. Think of the butcher shop they used to have on 34th and Seventh, right on the main floor. And the fish shop. When I worked there, they had an electronics brand called SupreMacy and every customer who bought one had the Macy's logo right there in their home every day and night. The bean counters got to them and analyzed it all away: Can't make money on electronics, can't compete with the electronics stores. Well, what if that wasn't the point? What if the point was to have our name in your home, as a trusted member of the family? How much is that worth?

"You know about the old-fashioned department stores," he told me. "They wouldn't exist today without the real estate they've grown up in over the years. The Macy's building on 34th Street? Think about Bloomingdale's on 59th. If they had to start today, they'd be boutiques. But they have this huge asset on their books, their buildings. It hides a multitude of sins. One day they'll have to sell them, or the air rights over them and we'll have condominiums where our great shopping worlds used to be."

Peter told me and I was shocked to learn that Macy's, home of the beloved parade and the official residence of Santa Claus in New York, has only just returned toys to the toy department. The store had given that up too, unable to compete with Toys 'R' Us and Wal*Mart on price and too unsure of how to contribute value beyond low price to the toy-buying moment.

When these stores were the vision of one person and existed in one specific place, the merchant's ear was to the ground. The salesperson knew both the merchandise and the customer. The buyer for the store, the person who traveled from Chicago or Peoria or San Francisco or Phoenix to New York to select and purchase the season's wares was buying for individual clientele. They had real people in mind. They were organized for individuality.

Today, the stores have gone in search of cost savings through efficiencies of scale. They are caught in a vice grip of ever thinner margins in order to compete with everyday low pricing, on one hand, while returning value to shareholders, as a publicly traded company, on the other. One of the major ways to save costs is to consolidate the buying offices.

Thus, Federated gobbles up Lord & Taylor, Marshall Field and more, and the inherent differences between the stores blur as one corporate buying group reporting to folks in the Cincinnati home office selects most everything, for all stores. The individual divisions (Macy's, Bloomingdale's, etc.) have ever fewer buyers searching for unique merchandise just for their shoppers, ever slighter "open to buy" discretionary lines on the balance sheet.

It is, I suppose, the very scale of an operation like Feder-ated that allows them to know and ignore the fact that each store, each customer and each sale must be treated differently. At these billion-dollar levels, they must create an accreditation program based on banal commonalities rather than the appeal of stark in-dividuality. There is no choice really for them, which means no choice for us either.

So who will educate the shopper if the stores refuse the mission and the salespeople aren't equipped? A new breed of magazine has stepped up to fill this void, at least partially.

"I think it's fair to say the radical success of our shopping magazines is, at least in part, due to the fact that we arose to fulfill the editorial need no longer being filled by individual store buy-ers," Rick Levine, who played a major role in the launch of *Lucky,* and then *Cargo* (for men), which didn't make it, and most recently *Domino* (for home) at Condé Nast, tells me.

Thus, *Lucky,* launched in 1999, is a spectacular publishing success story. Condé Nast has a robust magazine when it has a mil-lion in paid circulation and 1,000 pages of advertising. *Lucky* is way ahead of plan, because it met a need in the marketspace be-fore anyone else understood it was there. It came into being just as the consolidation of the department store chains—and most im-portant, their buying offices—was moving into warp speed.

The magazines simply showcase the "must have" fashion fea-tures of the moment, with a range of options in every price range. Sixty-two newsboy caps! Forty-four messenger bags! Twenty-seven desk lamps! Thirty-three cell phones! It shows the entire breadth of wares available, deconstructs the various elements, ex-plains the specific features of each offering—what you're getting, what you're giving up as you move up or down the price chain—and provides where-to-buy information. It's like a great depart-ment store, clerk and delivery service built into a publication.

"Our market editors go out and shop the country," Levine explains. "We had to invent a new system for getting the goods into the magazine in real time. Our market editors are out there, see the stuff, call it in, get it shot and into next month's issues, with information on where and how to get it. We are the ultimate in service."

Real Simple provides a comparable service in a different manner: Want to know about cashmere? They'll take you all the way back to the specific goats and all the way through the intricacies of single, double, triple-ply varietals. There's more to it than meets the hand when you reach out to touch it in the store, but no way to know that without being taught. We're not born with this information, we have to acquire it. The magazine *W* is yet one more way to get smart about the details of fashion and signals of profound quality.

Well, somebody had to see the *Shopportunity!* One great leap forward for publishing, but one giant missed opportunity for these once essential retailers.

When I worked with Waldenbooks, one of the things they worried about was people coming into their stores in a mall, deciding to buy a book, getting ready to write a check and then looking up and asking the salesperson, "Is this Walden or Dalton?" In other words, the books were exactly the same so there was nothing to differentiate one store from the other.

That's what is happening here. Some stores will rise to the challenge. They will grapple with the deep individuality available in the retail triangle: the shopper is unique, the salesperson is unique and the merchandise is unique. This has the potential to create a unique and intensely valuable experience: One, as Lillian Gilbreth put it, which results in a shopper who "must like herself better at the end of the transaction."

This all gives rise to Rule #11: The stuff is just stuff without the people to present it to shoppers. We must demand sales staff who know more than we do about the merchandise, about the details. We want people to contribute talent, value and care to the experience.

Rule #11: Shop Where the Staff Knows More than You

And Rule #12: Shop one level above your budget; it's free, after all. Educate yourself by going to the designer clothing floor of your best local department or specialty store. Investigate, ask questions. Who knows? Something you like may legitimately go on sale. A sales clerk may actually decide to call you and let you know. But at least you'll know the details to look for when you're sorting through the "bargains" at your usual store. You'll be able to tell the real from fake *Shopportunity!* And that's a grand thing.

Rule #12: Shop above Your Budget

Now, come away with me for a shopper's tour of Nyack. Yes, Nyack, and then to SoHo.

Eight

The Specialty of Specialty?
Why, Specialty!

The drumbeat of news was getting louder. Gap was creating a new retail store just for boomer women. Chico's had proven the merit of the market. It has grown to nearly 700 stores and topped $1 billion in sales by offering women 35-plus comfortable clothing in sizes from 1 to 3. Now Gap was going after this group as only Gap could. And so, off I went to Nyack to see for myself the prototype store, named Forth & Towne.

It is apparently the same "four shopper" stereotyping that Federated has discovered that is behind Gap's launch of Forth & Towne, a name meant to evoke a small-town retailer, but has already been christened with the subversive acronym FAT. One can imagine Katherine, Julie, Erin and Alex quite happily ensconced here, perhaps living nearby in a cul-de-sac in Nyack. Boomer women are the now aging group that first embraced Gap culture. But Gap's research shows these women have become put off by its teen jean couture.

J.C. Penney has stumbled upon these same four divisions of women, too. It's a little eerie to learn that all these merchants are trying to wrestle the radical differences among us into four discrete types in order to push clothes at us according to some logic system. Clothes designed and marketed to these "four types of women" will end up looking essentially more alike than different, of course. The evolution of fashion, which so wants to be kicky, edgy and unique, slouches instead toward sameness and predictability, all the while reducing our options and making the process much less adventurous and rewarding.

Entering the 8,000-square-foot Forth & Towne store, you are confronted with Federated's thinking in real space: To the left is the businesswoman's realm (traditional), to the right, the Eileen Fisher wannabe area (neotraditional). In the back left is all the stuff you remember from the original Gap (contemporary), in the right rear is merchandise for a first date, presumably after a first marriage or two has expired (fashion)—all, however, arrayed in sizes from 2 to 20.

And that sizing claim is a big one. A friend of mine who is essentially the same weight today as she was 25 years ago confesses that without taking off a pound she's moved effortlessly from a size 10 Gap jean into an 8. Why? Because, they are making them larger and in the process helping us deny that we are indeed making ourselves larger.

The one real innovation at Forth & Towne, and it is significant, is the return to the gorgeous fitting rooms of old. These rooms are so important that they actually comprise the center of the store, wrapped in a circle around a truly inspired conceit: a circular display piece that showcases accessories. Right there, where you're trying on the clothes, the sales clerk can easily lay hands on shoes, belts and bags.

Gap is planning on fine-tuning these stores and then rolling them out to many malls throughout the land. In these early showcase venues, the inventory is deep, the sales staff professional, courteous and hospitable, the sale signs nonexistent, the programs innovative. Bring in items from your wardrobe on Tuesday afternoons and they'll work with you to freshen them with new accessories. Want a bottled water? The Forth & Towne brand of water is at the ready.

The architectural detailing is there, but suspect. A high, hip stainless steel desk carries a styled and grouped collection of coffee table books. There are stools to sit on and browse, but the stools are too high for the desk. The look is right; the invitation to browse is something borrowed from a Barnes & Noble or Borders, but is not sincere.

It seems mean-spirited to quibble at such an earnest effort, but it's a weirdly lobotomized experience, shopping this store. It is not exciting. The heart does not leap up. It's so respectful, so willing to please, with its cheery sales staff, who seemingly fall into the size 8 to 10 area of an accurate sizing chart and appear to be a good decade or so younger than the age of the ideal shopper. It is the mass produced quality that takes the edge off the experience, I realize. When you're trying to make decisions not for one store but ultimately for hundreds, it requires a rounding of the edges that great retailers and designers simply don't have to do. Or perhaps once didn't have to do.

In the end, I leave without having purchased anything, although I am the shopper they are reaching out to. Though I was intent on analyzing it, I was open to buying something if the spark lit. It is too studied for me, too purposeful. I want my options more helter-skelter, my shopping more of an adventure. I have grasped their logic too neatly. There is nothing to discover. I shop on, pretty sure that Gap has some work to do on this concept before it takes this show to the mall.

• • •

Specialty retailing is tough. It evolved as a deeper, more specific experience than a department store could offer. The historic department stores sold everything from appliances to estate jewelry. Specialty stores focus on one or two elements, such as apparel or home décor. The rationale is that they can go deeper into the merchandise and they can hire and train salespeople who are more knowledgeable. Certainly in some categories, like bookselling, the theory goes, you get people who are writing their novels at night to serve as your guide during the daytime, or graduates of the Fashion Institute of Technology to host your *Shopportunity!* at Barneys, DKNY, the Gap, Abercrombie & Fitch, Ralph Lauren or Tommy. In other words, passionate, engaged professionals. It's an attractive construct in theory. In practice, it's a little less compelling. In most stores, it's episodic at best.

We are taking a specialty shopping tour of SoHo. I have lured Peter Connolly into the city from the horse country of New Jersey, asking him to walk around the neighborhood and tell me what he sees. He's Charlene's opposite number. If she's a shopper's shopper, he's a merchant's merchant. We go to Bloomingdale's in SoHo, it's deserted, but it's the Monday after Thanksgiving at 11 a.m. Just the fact of a Bloomies in SoHo is an exciting move for Federated to make. But it's a smaller store by far than the original at 59th and Lexington. Very pared down. Peter grins. The store's size makes his real estate point for him. The old, huge showcases are just no longer feasible. This is far more boutique than department store.

We go into a store called Mexx, which he points out has a problem with its windows: You can't see in. A real no-no in retailing terms, because it means the shopper may not even enter, unsure of what the interior holds.

"It's clearly for a 30- to 40-year old woman," he tells me. "Even the men's stuff is for her to buy for him. It's a look, a way of merchandising that allows her to touch everything; women like to touch stuff. It's for a woman who's working and living with her boyfriend, who is probably at an ad agency or in some creative field. She'd be at home here."

Next, we move into a no-name jewelry store.

"This is fabulous," he tells me. "Very narrow focus, but very deep. My daughter would love this. All costume, but fun. Silver stuff all together, then gold, then the bling. And you know it from even a glance inside. No surprises. It is just what it seems to be. Easy to shop."

We wander up and down streets and side streets, following our fancies in terms of which shops to enter and which to pass up. He tsk-tsks over a jeans store called Yellow Rat Bastard, not as I do because of the name and how to explain it to my daughter as she begins to read, but because of the jeans in the window with the price tags attached. "Look what Calvin has done to his brand," he moans to me. "Two pairs for $69, right there with the Wranglers."

Anthropologie? "Doesn't make sense to me, but I guess it's working," he tells me. We both hypothesize that this store is kind of a little SoHo, all on its own, with its wooden floors and raw architectural details that scream SoHo loft, with its eclectic merchandise that moves seamlessly from orange blossom–scented candles to blouses to lamps to hair ribbons to pants to costume jewelry. It explains the store's appeal here, but one wonders at how and why it works in a mall, although it may well work for the very same reason, of course. But, we have to take its appeal as an article of faith right now. There are no customers in the store.

Then, we get to one of his alma maters, Ralph Lauren. We enter the store on West Broadway and it's like we've been returned to the world of the living. The place is chockablock with people, shoppers, salespeople and merchandisers. It feels comfortably crowded and exciting. They are putting up the winter scene in the store. The manikins have faces here; they are not headless wonders. In fact they have expressions. They seem interested in what they're doing, even if it's just pretending to be on the ski slopes. They are engaged. We all are.

Midstore, the display people have arranged a little conversation pit right in the center of the room: no merchandise, just split-rail couch and chairs with white canvas cushions designed to offer respite, either après ski, in this imaginary world we've entered, or for the very real world of shopper exhaustion. It is a welcoming, gracious, stylish gesture.

It is here too that we are asked for the first time this day, "Do you need help?" I have become so accustomed to the profound indifference of sales help that I didn't really register this moment, but Peter underscores it: "Did you hear that?" he asks me. "Look! How long have we been at this? An hour and a half? Nine different stores? And here's the first one where somebody deigns to notice us."

Well, let's face it. Ralph knows what he's doing. He makes shopping his store a transformational experience. He's creating a mood, a moment, a memory. According to Peter, the merchandising looks for Ralph Lauren stores are done individually with understanding and respect for the architectural realities and the neighborhood nuances. There's also a playbook that shows when all the merchandise will be arriving, so that individual store managers can plan how best to showcase sweaters as they arrive one day from Italy and sheets as they arrive the next from France. The look stays the same for the week, but it's different every day: a living breathing organism we enter into.

We can clearly imagine a shopper's quest being fulfilled here wonderfully: *Anticipation, pursuit, prominence* and *appreciation* are all palpable. Everyone I speak with afterward has a story to tell me about Ralph Lauren anything. The shopping experience is a memorable one, one that shoppers love to relate: a suit for a first job interview, a shirt and jeans for a date, the desperate search for a tie for Father's Day—each purchase the stuff of personal history.

Peter believes that there's one merchandising director for this store and one for Madison Avenue. Two full-time visual display pros, plus their staffs, at the top of their games are creating this intensity, this allure. The depth of detail is incredible. Everywhere you look, you want to keep on looking. Salespeople attend to the needs of the customers, illustrating the hidden joys of some of the jacket features, or the way to fold the pocket square precisely. The sales process is part of the performance quality: It belongs here, not hidden, nor furtive, but relished by buyer and seller alike.

And the sale signs are there, too: Dignified, printed in what seems to be an ecru ink on dark green poster board, they are framed in wood, covered in glass. The "sale" is confined to what is clearly last season's merchandise. Charmingly, a pair of knee-high boots marked as on-sale are featured on a manikin. You don't believe you're getting factory seconds or that there's something sordid going on. Even the sale goods are part of the show.

We are sad to leave. We're moving out of a rarefied, *Shopportunity!* atmosphere and into the noon of the living dead. Next stop, Tommy's store, where his upscale H line is in full array. But really nothing now will compete successfully with Ralph. The store is empty. One store clerk recognizes Peter and asks him how it's going. There are black-and-white photos of New York on the wall; there is a large-scale painted wooden *H* on a bookcase every so often, but there is no joy in Mudville.

The center section of the store is being repainted a dark red; as shoppers we feel in the way of the guys toting the ladders and bustling around in overalls. "There should be a sign saying, 'Excuse us while we improve your shopping experience,' " Peter tells me, loudly enough to be overheard and ignored. We follow a sign that says, Women's, 31 Steps Upstairs. It seems easy enough to walk the 31 steps, but once there, not much point. This giant is sleeping. We leave.

We go into the new John Varvatos shop. It is gorgeous and

filled with spectacular menswear. Whether it's because of the lushness of the fabric or the care of the staff, there are no packing wrinkles on these clothes. They look perfect to the eye, and we both reach out just to touch them. The feel of the overcoat on the hand is extravagant.

This store, too, is deserted of shoppers. The staff seems made up half of sales clerks, and half of bouncers left over from a hot nightclub. The big beefy guys standing on the periphery look surly to be sure, but perhaps they suggest that there's something valuable here, not to be messed with, just as a security guard in front of Cartier serves the twofold purpose of protecting and positioning what's inside. Peter is not sure the technique works here.

We really can't go on, at this point. The wild ride inside Ralph has sort of ruined whatever comes next. Once you've been there, there is no going back. So we head to Cipriani for lunch, before going our separate ways.

Had there been one more store I could have whisked him to, it would have been Title 9, run by Missy Park. Named for the legislation that gave rise to the leap forward in girls' athletics in grade and high schools, Title 9 started out as a jog bra company. Like many entrepreneurial ventures, its genesis is rooted in Missy's own frustrations. As a college jock and marathon runner, she and her female colleagues at Yale were constantly irritated by the moment of entering a sporting goods store to search for a bra that worked in sports. Finding it was one thing, finding one of the male clerks to wait on them was something else entirely.

So she figured out a method for fitting bras by phone. And with that, she was up and running as a women's sporting wear catalog company. After a decade or so, she decided to try her hand at retail and now there are seven Title 9 stores, in California, Colorado and Oregon.

When she interviews new hires, she doesn't ask them about their career goals, she asks them about their sports goals. She hires women who are amateur athletes and want to work most of the year, but need to take a leave of absence for the occasional triathlon. She doesn't give them rules or manuals for how to stock, staff or merchandise the stores; she hires people who are passionate about women's sports and then she lets them do their thing.

"The manager of our Boulder store is a case in point," she tells me. "She's a marathoner. A woman comes into the store and they engage in conversation. She learns that the woman has just begun to run marathons and she's looking for an all-weather-gear set to run in the next weekend. Rain has been forecast.

"The manager tells her not to bother. She says, 'If you buy that, you'll want to take it off after the first few miles and then you won't know what to do with it.' So, she reaches down under the counter and pulls out a big black garbage bag. She cuts armholes in it and tells the woman to wear that. By the time she's hot from running, she'll be able to tuck it into the back of her shorts and keep running, or pass it off to someone on the route."

Missy is not only okay with giving up this sale, she's proud of it. It's exactly what she believes is first, the right thing to do, rather than to sell inappropriate merchandise to a novice, but also the smart thing to do. "Where else will this woman ever shop?" she asks me. And, of course, she's right.

It's good to note that this is very different from giving that woman 15 percent off for opening a store charge or 30 percent off on a purchase she didn't need. Here, the salesperson is providing a genuine education; she is wildly knowledgeable, not just about the product, but about its ultimate purpose. She knows women's sports. She trusts that Missy is in this for the long haul, not today's or this week's or this quarter's sales numbers. Indeed, Missy is running a privately-held company; she doesn't need to "make her numbers" to please the street this quarter. She needs to build a relationship with her salespeople and her customers through her merchandise and sometimes the best way to do that is not to sell. Thrilling, really.

Ordering from her catalog is another excellent adventure. If the people on the phone aren't sure which size bra is exactly right for you, they send you two with a postage-paid return mailer. Pick the one you like and send the other back. No hassle. She also has an environmental ethic that isn't articulated but that screams through her shipping department. Order merchandise from her and it comes in the smallest package possible, no packing peanuts to fret with.

The models in her catalog are real female athletes, many of whom are longtime friends of the people of Title 9. Missy herself writes the catalog copy. It's all honest, clear and done to Missy's personal standards. "Just shoot me if I ever tell you I've had to do a focus group to figure out what my customers want," she tells me, laughing.

So, of course, we go back to Rule #10: Shop with people who know more about the product than you do. But also, Rule #13: Follow the passion. Someone who spends their spare time in competitive athletics is far more likely to care deeply about getting you the right stuff than a minimum-wage sneaker salesman in a mall. Someone who is passionate about the details in fashion, like Ralph, is likely to attract people to him who are obsessed as well. How do you think your salesperson, or indeed the owner of the shop, spends their spare time?

Rule #13: Follow the Passion

Now, isn't it time to eat—and to visit our local supermarket?

Nine

Food Shopping?
The Best of Times.
The Worst of Times.

Created just 75 years ago, in August 1930 in Queens, New York, the supermarket began life as bouncy baby King Kullen, a 1,000-item shop. Today, it is the bloated, dirty, frontline of a class war pitting the mercilessly underpaid staff, rarely able to afford to live anywhere near these bastions of consumption, against their convenience seeking, overwrought, ready-to-pounce customers. Grocery stores in blue-collar or working-poor neighborhoods are just that much dirtier, grimier and sullen. Add to that mix the frequent accusation that absentee owners price-gouge local patrons who have no shopping options outside the neighborhood.

In this country we evaluate food not by its freshness, not by its evocative transformational power—from mere ingredients into powerful family meaning and memories—and not by its nutrition, but by its price. The signs on the windows, the circulars in the papers, the annoying announcements over the store's public address system all conspire to communicate cheap, cheaper and cheapest. The price of a six-pack of Coca-Cola or a pound of chuck is the sole criteria upon which we're meant to evaluate the store.

The world of the supermarket is ridiculously outmoded. Manufacturers work hard to prop it up, in order to have somewhere to sell, beyond Wal*Mart. The state of today's grocery shopping is just one of the sad, unintended consequences of everyday low prices. There is no money to improve the experience: Everyone must slather their windows with promotions aimed at convincing you that cheap food is what you crave.

Let's just think about it for a moment. If an airline said to you, "Fly less with us, we'll treat you better. We'll whisk you in and out of the airport faster," you'd say, "Great, but that's not really fair to your frequent fliers, is it?" We just naturally know that the best treatment should go to the people who spend the most, right? Well, welcome to the topsy-turvy world of grocery shopping.

If you have 11 items, you can stand on line for hours. So, you learn quickly to buy fewer than 10 items and receive preferential treatment. You learn, indeed, to stash that 11th item in the magazine rack by the checkout counter where a stock boy is going to have to find it and return it to its rightful place at some point. Or perhaps you learn that the cashier won't notice you're over your limit, so you can sneak in a couple of extra purchases, hoping the person behind you doesn't rat you out.

However, if you want to spend $150 with the store, well fine, wait here, the store's logic dictates. Just resign yourself to an extra 20 minutes or so. Since you're trying to spend a lot of money with us, we're just going to have to penalize you, aren't we? What a goofy business model.

I must confess I have not gone into a conventional grocery store since 1985. Walking around a Murray Hill Gristedes on Lexington Avenue one day, I had a vision. I suddenly saw the dirt, the grime, the harshness of the fluorescent lights, the hostility, all of it together as if for the first time and I thought, life is too short—I'll figure out some other way. This being New York, it's relatively easy to go to the (albeit equally filthy) corner deli for milk, beer and Dorito chips, place a daily order at the corner diner for coffee and cheese danish, rely on Japanese, Chinese, Mexican and pizza places to deliver, and convince the local dry cleaner to do laundry. It really wasn't that difficult. And, for those occasions when I wanted to entertain, I could use a caterer or invite friends over for drinks and then go out to dinner. In short, I learned to cope, albeit at a cost. Not just the fees associated with my grocery store avoidance system, but the loss of joy. I did not select fresh produce, know when it was cherry season, engage in conversation with the fishmonger, read and try recipes from the newspaper, or discover new spices. The smell of fresh-made soups did not permeate my home for decades.

Out-of-town friends told me for years that the problem was New York City grocery stores. I needed to visit suburbia. I said, okay, but I'm not going alone. I invited myself to Atlanta and asked Ian Rattray and his partner, Tom Magness, to take me around. They design retail stores and I wanted to see through their very educated eyes.

I asked to see the best and worst of what this world has to offer. The best because I was on the hunt for a way out of the death spiral of price in this profoundly commoditized world. Was the joy of food celebrated anywhere? The worst, because I wanted to understand the signals, the signs that we can read from the road to ward off even one ghastly food shopping excursion.

We started with the worst: A store called Edward's IGA in the Briarcliff area of Atlanta. Let's begin from the outside in. We're in a strip mall and ours is one of three cars in the entire lot. The *s* in

Edward's has fallen off the sign; the accumulated rust on the sign suggests its fall was not recent. Four streetlights meant to illuminate the parking lot are broken. You can't see inside, because of the huge signs screaming price: Rump Roast, $3.99 a pound! Tide, $4.99! Land o' Lakes Butter, $3.29 a pound! Ian tells me that taken all together, this is store code for "drop dead."

We enter. Everywhere there are "danglers," the signs that hang from the ceiling and also scream price. These danglers have been given to the store by the manufacturers. Some proclaim the value of Kraft brands, others are handed out by Procter & Gamble, still others by Chiquita and Dole. The signs say something banal at the bottom, like "A Century of Value," and show the company's logo. The big white space is filled up with the news that macaroni and cheese is five for $4.99.

After we get acclimated to the omnipresence of the danglers, we see that the neighborhood notice board is empty: nobody is offering piano lessons; there are no church socials or street fairs being advertised here. The floors are filthy and there are boxes, cut open and sitting empty in the aisles. The produce is dirty; it has a film on it that is dusty to the touch.

"This store suffers from a lack of love," says Ian. "They don't love their merchandise, they don't love their customers." He points to a handwritten sign on the door to the back room: "No public restrooms. Do not enter." Tom nods and gestures to the convex mirrors at every corner of the store. They are the kind most typically installed on winding roads to help motorists see what's coming around the bend. "They don't trust their shoppers or their employees," he explains. "The mirrors help the manager keep the whole store in view so he can make sure nobody pockets anything."

These are messages we can read from far off. If your store has a shoddy parking lot, huge price-touting signs blocking vision in (or out) of the store, dangling signs screaming price some more once you're in the door, no public restrooms and traffic mirrors to help an aloof manager monitor you and his employees, run, don't walk, in the opposite direction. You don't need to go farther down this road, although we soldiered on.

We walk up the coffee aisle. The dispensers where the fresh beans should be are empty, except for a few ancient, orphaned beans that refused to abandon their plastic home. The little plastic packets of artificial creamers in many different flavors are right where they ought to be, next to the coffee, but, weirdly enough, after them come Huggies. The salty snacks snuggle next to the Clorox. The Raid roach killer is ensconced next to the Frito-Lay chips and pretzels. The toothpaste section is adjacent to the pencils and notebooks.

"Everywhere you look," Ian says whirling around, "you see a sea of yellow and yellow is the color of discount. It blazes through here. Look at the booze, all yellow signs, all about price—and look at the brands and the sizes: wino sizes, half gallons of cheap wine."

We move through the frozen section. It would be dusty too, if it weren't frostbitten. The area seems positively smoky as the refrigerated air meets the warmth of the store. Everything has a layer of frost on it. No longer food, it seems to have sat here untouched by human hands for months and turned slowly into anonymous lumps. The layer of frost renders each package inscrutable. The signs that explain the price and the contents of each refrigeration case do not correlate easily to the products. You know somewhere there are Aunt Jemima waffles for $1.29, but where? You see the frozen orange juice in the case, but how much is it?

"Forget love," says Ian. "There's not even romance in this store. Nothing is mechandised to make you want to buy it. The store is out of control. The manufacturers give them the signs and probably put them up for them. There is nothing that tells you

you're at Edward'_IGA once you're in the store. They've given it over to the manufacturers, probably because they don't want to have to pay their people enough to put up and change their own signs."

Ian and Tom think this is a family-owned store nestled between a really affluent neighborhood and one that is more mainstream middle class. There are beautiful homes in the area, but also some large apartment complexes.

"The father or even grandfather probably started here and the kids are doing just enough to eek out a living," they agree. "It won't make it to the next generation." Meanwhile, I have seen nothing, of course, to alter my vision of grocery shopping. So we move on. Toward the light.

Whole Foods may be old news, but it is still a beautiful thing to behold. Amazingly, we're only a mile or so from Edward'_IGA. But we are light-years away. The parking lot is full; we wait for someone to leave in order to claim their space.

We walk up and the profusion of seasonal merchandise, pumpkins, apples, and mums welcomes us before we even get inside. The store is simply sumptuous; there is no other word. Such abundance, so much choice—and something more. A Missy Parkesque ethic beckons. Just as she celebrates the joy of sports for women, and well-designed apparel as simply a means to that end, Whole Foods reminds us of the wonder of food, how it begins as mere ingredients and is transformed into nourishment and from there into hospitality, love—and memories.

The store features locally grown organic food. Nothing bad or irresponsible lurks here. It also features a knowledgeable, committed staff who love their wares. Want to know where the rutabagas are? No problem. Any earnest staffer will not just point in the general direction, but will escort you there. The romance, indeed the love of food, is clear.

"I once was looking for a certain kind of melon," Ian tells me, proud of this place. "They were out. A produce clerk comes over and asks me if I need help. He's seen me searching the aisles for what had been here last week. I tell him. He tells me, 'You know, I like those too, but we couldn't get any this week that met our standards. But there's another type of melon I tried, which tastes wonderful and quite like yours.' And right then and there, he takes one from the pile and slices it open, with a knife he has with him. He offers me a piece to evaluate. Of course, it was delicious and I bought three—and I learned to love a different kind of melon."

We are in love with this story. It hits all the right *Shopportunity!* notes. Discovery, of course, but also a sales clerk who knows that it's perfectly appropriate and indeed encouraged to break open the inventory (no one sits on high to spy on us from a Lucite enclosed booth, surrounded by highway mirrors). Ian describes the employees as embracing the "dude quality of the store." They are savvy, in-the-know and seem committed, in a laid-back, cool kind of way.

All around the section there are signs and large-scale, easily read, stenciled statements on the walls attesting to the Whole Foods ethic. "We support organic farmers, growers and the environment through our commitment to sustainable agriculture and by expanding the market for organic products." Their mission is part of what we're buying and buying into. Price promotion does not rear its ugly head.

Want to know about heirloom tomatoes? Purple Cherokee, Arkansas Traveler, Marvel Stripe, Mortgage Lifter, Brandywine? To be considered an heirloom, a tomato must have been grown from seed that has produced the same variety of tomato going back at least until 1940. Wow!

Interested in cheese? Ask for a taste before you buy. Hundreds are artfully arranged for your viewing and sampling pleasure. What about olives? How about Arbequinas, the popular Spanish olive. Or Beldi, from Morocco. Or Bitetto, with its "delicate fruitiness and almond tones." Perhaps the Cerignola, harvested north of Bari in the Puglia region of Italy, or the Gaeta, "fun to snack on but difficult to pit for recipes," or the Halkidiki, "the tangy green olive grown only on Greece's Halkidiki peninsula." We're only to *H* in the alphabet of olives.

The signs around the produce section, the cheese section, the wine area, indeed everywhere, are there to educate, to tutor us in the features of each product, and oh, by the way, its cost. Of course, each thing is going to be a bit more expensive: It's rare, it's evocative, it's ethical. Even the "Whole Body" section is filled with shampoos, conditioners, soaps and moisturizers that required no meanness to animals to create. You just feel great about each and every purchase.

Where Edward'_IGA had empty cut boxes in the aisles, here the aisles are interrupted with convincing wooden crates, authentic-appearing vestiges of small-farm shipping realities. They may be merchandising tools now, but they showcase the food naturally. There are no manufacturer signs anywhere. It is all about Whole Foods. We can feel the trust sink in: These people know what they're doing.

Small wonder it's the fastest growing grocery chain in the country. Okay, so there are only 177 stores and it can lay claim to only one percent of the market. Still, it's alive. It's growing. It's exhilarating. Meanwhile, Winn-Dixie has gone bankrupt, Albertsons has sold itself, and Kroger and Safeway are stagnating, their profits bleak.

But here, in Whole Foods, there are a thousand details to admire: 18-inch deep shelves vs. the industry standard 24-inch ones. Why? Because they don't want the merchandise to be stocked once a week and left to deplete itself. More efficient perhaps, but, well, ugly. They want their stock people to go through, day by day, and hour by hour, ensuring packages are easy to reach—and easier to see.

The polished cement floor elicits oohs and ahhs from Ian and

Tom: It's a hard (and expensive) surface to create correctly, but once you've got it right, it can be cleaned easily and often with a wet mop—and oh! how it gleams and reflects the light issuing from the beautiful, nearly theatrical quality of the lighting fixtures. Not for Whole Foods shoppers or merchandise the grim fluorescence of more common stores.

Whole Foods must hire people with an aesthetic sensibility. It isn't simple to stack two dozen pears in a pyramid. I bet they screen for patience, too, since the leaning tower of peaches must be reconstructed time after time. Somehow they find employees eager to artfully arrange cheeses on a platter. It's a gift to get the produce to spill out of the merchandising cornucopia in a joyous Thanksgiving homage that would be at home in the pages of *Martha Stewart Living.*

I go for the torture test: the restrooms. Yes, of course, you're welcome to use them. They are clean, tidy, utilitarian. They are located where you can actually find them. You're not exactly encouraged to dawdle or converse with a fellow shopper, but there's a café for that purpose. Even the places in the store that are off-limits to shoppers are politely off-limits: Team Members Only, the sign reads. It kind of makes you want to apply to work there. And why not? It's on *Fortune*'s list of the 100 Best Companies to Work For.

The hand-lettered quality of the signs amaze. Tom, Ian and I are obsessed with wondering how they do it. They seem to be chalk boards, with wonderful handwriting in various chalky colors. Does each store hire a calligrapher? Well, no. Ian leaps up to touch one. The letters are made from stickers, like Mattie has to tell Barbie stories. The sticker words are then applied to the chalk boards. It conveys spontaneity, as if announcing today's specials based on what's just arrived. But they figured out how to deliver the look more easily, predictably and affordably than scribes in the back room could do.

Real music is playing, interesting music, not the creepy Muzak that shadowed us at Edward'_IGA. "The human ear loves the familiar," explains Ian, as we realize we're smiling to hear Janis Ian and then Tony Bennett and then the Beatles and then a cut of World Music. The mix is thoughtful, friendly, interesting. "The human eye loves the new," he tells me, and sure enough I'm looking on in wonder at frozen dog food shipped in from New Zealand. Fascinating. Perhaps I should get Mattie a dog for her birthday.

The "adjacencies," as Ian calls them, are eminently logical here. There is brown rice near the sushi. There are more cheese boards near the wine section. And there are wines near the cheese section. The store is wonderfully intuitive to shop; you just amble along, following the thoughtful inevitability of the layout.

"It's an editorial premise," says Ian. "They are telling a story and we are walking through it." The narration tracks. And I am thinking, Why don't I shop at Whole Foods in New York? This is wonderful. This is a food *Shopportunity!* if ever there was one. I like the Whole Foods story.

Whole Foods is an exhilarating counterpoint to Edward'_ IGA, of course. This chain has a point of view. You may not want to embrace the organic ethic, but it's fair to ask that a point of view of some sort should be apparent. What is the store's reason for being? What does it care about? Where is its passion? A food *Shopportunity!* requires an ethic beyond cheap. If it's not there, drive on.

One of the great joys of working on this book has been meeting people who were willing to tell me their shopping stories. One such is the author and food memoirist Laura Schenone, who is also the wife of my editor, Herb Schaffner, and the mother of two marvelous boys, Gabriel and Simon. One night over dinner she described her own shopping rituals, and I was particularly in awe of her food shopping prowess.

As Laura explains it to me, she's working from a kind of topographical map of the local food geography. She can go deeply into her neighborhood to find the perfect loaf of olive bread, or just skim the surface by doing a quick fly-by the A&P. "One of the many reasons we chose Montclair is because we found a sort of foodiness to it that was exciting. I call it my mental map. Sure, I go to my local A&P for household basics, but I also go to Whole Foods for organic produce, meat, fish, dairy; I believe in the sustainability of our resources, so I believe in what they are doing. I also believe in personal relationships when I shop. So whenever I have the time, I go to one of two great local bakeries for bread. I figure bread is one of those wonderful items that's so delicious and so inexpensive, I don't need to economize here, I can be indulgent."

And then and then she goes to Paterson. Paterson, New Jersey, where the ingredients for wildly diverse ethnic foods can be found. "There's a basic gradation for me, a continuum between the ethics of a Whole Foods and the honest ethnicity of Paterson: Poles, Russians, Italians, Turks, everything is there, including passion. These people are passionate about food in the same raw way I am. I resonate to it; it makes me happy just to see it.

"I love the search for the red pepper paste I can't find anywhere else. The cheese, the nuts, the olives, the spinach pies I buy by the dozens to freeze and have whenever my sons ask for them; they just love them. It's gritty. It's not mass produced. Some of what I buy is amazingly cheap; some of it is very luxurious. I believe that great cooking is a combination of economy and luxury; it benefits from that interaction."

Because she's constantly thinking and writing about food and its origins and meaning, she's a credible resource to put it in succinct perspective for me: "A great motivation for the people who came to this country was the abundance of food here," she says. "Let's face it, a great many of our ancestors who immigrated here were hungry. The abundance of food in this country—and its low price—was nothing short of a miracle."

This miracle was transformed from that sheer raw profusion by the development of mass production. The assembly line may have been born from Henry Ford's efficiency expertise in making Model T's one after the other, but the extrapolation to the manufacture of food did not take long.

One baker could only make so many cookies in a day. But a factory? Well, a plant organized around an assembly line begins to spew out millions of cookies. It can, in fact, run 'round the clock, no one person knowing more than just their small compartmentalized task. See it there, the sugar, the wheat flour, the eggs, the milk, the powdered chocolate, the partially hydrogenated oil, slurried together in industrial vats to form the dough that will be force-fed into mechanized tubes, then spurted into cookie shape to slide along the slithering conveyor belts, whisked in, through and out of the ample ovens, jolted into paper sleeves before being ratcheted around and hurled into bright packages, brown cartons, warehoused on pallets and then shipped across the country.

Along the way, Laura explains, we began to believe in the superiority of foods made by machines, rather than people. "It's somehow cleaner and better to have a machine mass-produce your cookies than to have them made by a human being," she says, certain but mystified nonetheless.

It is precisely the "touched by a human being" element that she seeks as she shops. A visit to the Montclair Bread Company is just that, a visit. "I walk in and I ask about their kids, they ask about mine," she explains. "I know a little about the owner Sally's story, she knows something of mine. We talk—not a long time, but we know each other. I know her values. They make great earnest breads, organic breads, that are wonderful. Yes, they are more expensive than the supermarket, but on the scale of life's possible luxuries, this is a modest way to splurge?"

But some days you just don't feel like bearing the weight of the world on your bread, so Laura shops at another bakery, too, one that makes rich, indulgent loaves, perhaps with cinnamon and raisins, perhaps dates, perhaps olives. An adventure: What has the neighborhood baker dreamed up today?

It's a way of connecting to the world, she explains. Food is so primary, so essential. Perhaps today she'll go to Rosario's, the butcher, who will happily go out of his way to teach her about the pork butt, explaining that it comes from the shoulder. He'll sell her the special, imported flour she needs to make her own pasta.

For Laura, shopping goes beyond mere buying—and that is as it should be in a genuine *Shopportunity!* Always, she'll find something that goes beyond simple ingredients. She'll find people who are still "spiritually involved" with what they eat, shoppers and purveyors aligned in the belief that there is sustenance beyond calories, that there are nutrients in the memories and meaning of preparation, ritual, recipes handed down from one generation to the next, family, celebration and, well, food. Laura's engagement in the sheer excitement of the human experience of shopping is the antithesis of the typical.

I think of her as I read the obituary of Ruth M. Siems, the woman who invented Stove Top Stuffing. The final paragraph in the *New York Times* speaks volumes: "As a mark of just how deeply inscribed on the American palate Ms. Siems's stuffing has become, there are several recipes, available on the Internet, that promise to reproduce the taste of Stove Top from scratch, using fresh ingredients." That packaged, predictable taste, with its deep convenience allure, may have become the country's gold standard for stuffing, but not at Laura's home, I'll warrant.

I confess to being envious of Laura's tenacity. Of course, these kinds of markets must exist within walking distance of my apartment here in Manhattan. We are a stone's throw from Chinatown and Little Italy. I could, and think I should, re-create Laura's food-centric *Shopportunity!* But it seems daunting and irrefutably time-consuming. Nonetheless Laura's approach is a powerful one, delivering an emotional wallop. When I served my stock-in-trade pizza to Gabriel, Simon and Mattie, five-year-old Simon looked up at me quizzically. "Is this homemade?" he asked. Both Mattie and I were nonplussed. "It's from Raimo's, a great neighborhood pizzeria down the street," I told him." "Oh," he said, clearly embarrassed for us.

So there we are. I admire Laura's approach, and having my own child gives the emotional pull of "homemade" extra force, plus the nacho delivery guy strategy I'd pursued for so many years isn't all that healthy for a six-year-old. But I simply don't have Laura's essential resource: time. I need the convenience upon which the supermarket was built. Happily, technology is coming to my rescue.

Nearly a decade ago, when I was president of Faith Popcorn's BrainReserve, Faith and I were approached by a startlingly smart young man named Tim DiMello. He was starting a company in suburban Boston called Streamline. The idea came to him after he spent six months at home with his wife and kids. Tim had been amazed at how much time women spend doing the same thing over and over again.

Unlike Laura delighting in her quests, these women were heaving themselves up into their SUVs and driving to the ShopRite, then to the dry cleaners, then to the liquor store, then to the video rental store, then to the drug store, then to the photo shop and then home, on a twice weekly hamster wheel circuit. Tim felt this routine was beyond inefficient; it was abusive. So he went about the process of figuring out how to streamline their lives.

He hit upon the idea of first consolidating all these needs under one warehouse roof and then simply delivering it all to the women, once a week. But these were suburban women, no doorman standing at the ready to sign for packages, so he invented storage containers that would sit like lockboxes in their garages.

Only the customer and the bonded Streamline delivery man would have access.

The women entered their needs and their credit card numbers on a secure Website. Streamline's computers analyzed the orders, consolidating the individual desires into specific instructions to local farmers, dairies, toilet paper distributors, video rental companies, and on and on. The women would drop off their videos in the lockbox, along with film to be developed, empty bottles and cans to be recycled and clothes to be dry cleaned. "The Streamline man" would collect those when he dropped off the week's groceries. Poof! A new shopping ritual added hours to the days of these stay-at-home shoppers, just as Ivory soap had once liberated their grandmothers so long ago.

Faith and I both loved this concept. We knew Tim was onto something huge. Surely a cultural transformation was in the making. And, indeed, the customers loved it. There were soon reports of husbands and kids going online to the Streamline Website and adding to the lists. When was the last time husband or child volunteered for grocery store duty? Local real estate agents told Tim that suddenly people started asking to move into Streamline neighborhoods. Others refused to move from them, even if their spouses were offered a promotion. He had tapped the deep vein of a consumer's unmet need.

Procter & Gamble and a number of other companies had come to Boston to study the Streamline system, to understand if this was, indeed, the future of the grocery store. Our colleagues from P&G were not so sure about the richness of the vein, however. They told us that Tim's model wasn't "scalable." Kind of like the old adage that if you lose a nickel on every sale, you can't "make it up on volume," they argued that Streamline could never serve enough customers to reap big profits.

Tim's vision was 20/20; his model was bathed in red ink and so, after struggling mightily, Streamline succumbed in 2001 when the dot.com bubble truly burst. It simply had not been able to off-set the high costs of a start-up with enough business volume to sustain it. The lockboxes, the weekly delivery circuits, the heady array of services (dry cleaning! photos! videos!) beyond food. Everything that made the women's days an aching routine, made it difficult to, well, streamline.

It was an idea whose time had not yet come.

In 2003, I moved into Tribeca, historically a business district of the city, near Wall Street. It has only recently become even passingly residential (the name stands for "TRIangle BElow CAnal, an area hitherto known for its Army-Navy surplus stores). There was exactly one grocery store in the neighborhood, a Food Emporium, and I went to it, hoping against hope that the 17 years since last I ventured forth would have allowed for some progress to be made. Alas. It was the same dirty, grungy, begrudging place I'd remembered from my foray into that Gristedes on Lexington, so long before.

But I want to make a home for myself and my daughter now. What to do? There at the entrance to the Midtown Tunnel was the answer: A larger than life electronic billboard that looked like a fresh, inviting farmer's market times 100. Huge produce loomed. It was advertising something called FreshDirect.com.

I urge you to go to the site, even if you don't live in Manhattan. Plug in a Manhattan address and ZIP code and see the future for yourself. FreshDirect is Tim's home-delivery idea made workable by adding a single-minded obsession with the food, losing the sub-urban lockboxes and wandering delivery routes, choosing to focus on densely-populated urban areas (with doormen to accept delivery), and forgetting about dry cleaning, photo finishing or anything that takes your eye off the melon. Someone with a Laura-eyed view of food is behind this enterprise.

The first thing to notice is the name. The misstep that Tim made was in trying to brand a benefit: I will streamline your life.

Thus, the name frames the problem and the solution: Your life is a broken treadmill and I'm going to fix it. What FreshDirect says is "You want great food and we're the best in the world at getting it and bringing it to you." Great, fresh food, direct from the farmer. And that's what you get. FreshDirect bypasses the middleman, the distributors, the days in the warehouses, all of it. It both gets your food to you more quickly, so its wares are fresher, and it saves the expense of paying those middlemen, so you're not paying a steep premium for the genuine superiority, plus convenience. Voilà! FreshDirect is a growing business.

I didn't fully appreciate the difference between Tim's approach and FreshDirect's until I got my first order. I didn't use the lettuce the day I had planned to, and I was staggered a week later to see that the frisée was still fresh, appealing and begging for a dollop of goat cheese, some lardons and a swipe of salad dressing. It really was fresher food, delivered to my door.

In the Streamline model, the assumption was that we dislike shopping and want to avoid it. In the FreshDirect world view, we love the foods, we're fascinated by the artisanal cheese, thrilled by the Montauk Day Boat lobster and clam deliveries, eager for the organic plum season to arrive. FreshDirect gives us Lauraesque joys of discovery—who knew there was an organic plum season?—but without the profound investment of time her approach requires.

The FreshDirect man comes within a two-hour window of the time you request, but he can bring you things every day if you want him to. There's a modest delivery fee, a $40 minimum and a cut-off on ordering; you must place your order by 11 p.m. the night before. They do beautiful catering platters. They deliver great wines. The meat is stupendous. The fish could not be fresher—the produce either—and the ordering process is actually quite a bit of fun. At our house, the FreshDirect man arrives on Friday between 4 and 6 and we're set up for the week ahead.

FreshDirect is now a $100-plus million business. It boasts one expense line that conventional grocery stores never have: Six percent of sales or roughly $600,000 is budgeted for parking and traffic tickets as the drivers negotiate their way through the city. The service has expanded beyond Manhattan to include Brooklyn and Staten Island. It is delightfully designed for the eight million or so souls who live in New York City. Perhaps it, or something like it, will begin to invade other major American cities.

I am not alone in my aversion to grocery stores, of course. The Edward'_IGA is not just an isolated island of incompetence in Atlanta, either. Whole Foods isn't affordable for everyone. The gauntlet posed by grocery shopping in most American stores is a treacherous one for most of us, most of the time. Try going shopping with two preschoolers. Attempt to get service at the bakery counter. Ask a clerk stocking the shelves where the nail polish remover is.

But there are bright spots, even in the world of routine weekly grocery shopping. Everyone I spoke to who lives anywhere near a Wegmans, for example, is just euphoric about shopping there. At Wegmans the ethic seems to be the joy of food, plain and simple. It's not about organic, the way a Whole Foods is, but it deserves a special trip because it does provide all the promise of a supermarket's convenience with the elation of being among people who love what they do.

Peter Connolly, my specialty store shopping guru, is beyond enthusiastic about it. Everything they do is ripe with nuance. "Any other store when you buy wine they put it in a bag with cardboard dividers," he tells me. "It rattles and shakes around; you're at risk of the bag breaking as you carry it out. It's just awkward. At Wegmans they invented a really neat box with a handle to transport the wine you've bought. It is a very thoughtful experience. It treasures the product in a way that helps you respect it."

The Wegmans chain, family-owned out of Rochester, has over the past decade expanded into New Jersey and parts of New York.

It's not just family-owned, it's family run: Robert Wegman, recently deceased, was the visionary chairman. His son, Danny, is the CEO, and Danny's daughter, Colleen, is the president. I'm becoming a big proponent of nepotism because of them. With nearly $4 billion in annual sales, they have figured something out: Each year, nearly 4,000 communities petition Wegmans to put a store in their towns.

When they do open a new store, they put a store manager into the community fully a year and a half before the store opens, to determine the strengths and weaknesses of competition from the shopper's eye view, of course, but also so they can learn the nuances and values of the market.

According to a *Fortune* magazine report, Wegmans simply changed the gravitational laws that have thus far governed the grocery shopping experience, with "better quality goods, a spectacular abundance of choice, restaurant-quality prepared foods, beautiful stores and displays, and a nearly telepathic level of customer service." All delivered at a fair price.

That telepathic level of customer service is, of course, what amazes. There are wooden trims to the refrigeration cases, which just take the edge off and warm up the entire place. There are the large, clearly printed aisle and shelf markers that make the experience intuitive. There are the clean, actually well-scented restrooms easily found right at the front of the store, and the For Your Convenience area that allows you to pop in and out for a gallon of milk. But there is also the sign you notice only on the way out that promises curb-to-car umbrella service by Wegmans staff people to help you on rainy days.

It all ratchets up to an almost overwhelming feeling that Wegmans honors its food, its customers and its employees equally. There is a respect here that just pervades the experience.

Wegmans promises 70,000 products, compared to an average of just over 40,000 in most supermarkets. Cheese? There are more than 400 specialty cheeses at any one time. And all this is not crammed into the typical grocery store "footprint." Rather they have spacious aisles and 80,000 to 120,000 square feet of wander room. Want to deal with your dry cleaning? But of course. Need prescriptions filled? No problem. Film developed? Step right up. Flowers? Greeting cards? How about a wok? It's all here. It's all fairly priced. It's grocery store nirvana.

Tired and want to pause? Try the Market Café, with seating for 100 to 200 shoppers. Of course there's a wide variety of pre-pared foods, sushi, pizza and wings, garden fresh salads. And a coffee bar with the *de rigueur* cappuccino. But there's also a Kids Fun Center, where children from three to eight can play, while their parents shop.

In ambience, Wegmans is more like a European open-air mar-ket: Their Website describes "displays of fresh-caught seafood, meat, deli products and imported cheeses, international foods—plus all the foods and household items usually found in supermar-kets." They couple this with "dazzling displays of fresh produce, artisan breads and other baked goods hot from the oven several times a day."

The bakery is an important element. There are bakers here. They really are baking *in the store.* Huge Hobart ovens provide the backdrop, augmented by industrial strength floor-standing mixers. The profusion of fresh breads, pies, cookies, cakes cooling on rolling racks and then lovingly arrayed in display cases rivals anything I can find in my neighborhood.

I interviewed women about the in-store bakeries at their local supermarkets. "Oh, when they started out it was fine," they agreed. "I loved the smell when you'd walk in the door," one re-called. But pretty quickly, the stores decided to shave costs: The baking is actually done in an industrial bakery that provides for all the stores in a chain. The baked goods are just delivered daily to the stores and they spray the area with "fresh baked" smells.

"It ruined it for me," one woman recalled, "when I saw that the guy behind the counter today wearing the chef's hat was the same guy who bagged my groceries last week." Now, these "bakeries" are simply the desperate answer for harried mothers who forgot it was their turn to bring treats to the Brownie or Cub Scouts meeting.

"The stuff comes on a plastic platter, it's usually got brightly colored icing on it and the kids don't really know the difference," the woman told me. "It's fine. It will do. But for anything important, or when I'm not in a hurry, I go to a good bakery across town."

Perhaps at most supermarkets, but surely not at Wegmans.

Perhaps the most important difference between Wegmans and a typical supermarket is felt rather than seen, experienced rather than advertised. There's a genuine career path for their associates. At Wegmans, the baker is actually a baker. Go back next week and you're quite likely to find him there—and he most likely will remember you, too. You'll have that touch of humanity that Laura craves, right there in a supermarket.

So if Wegmans is the model of how good it can be, why isn't everybody stealing its ideas? Follow the money: If the store is part of a chain that is part of a publicly-traded corporation, then it is being evaluated by stock analysts on earnings and on sales growth in stores open more than a year. In order to have Wall Street pundits applaud your earnings and "comp store sales" numbers, you must move lots of goods cheaply, pay people as little as possible and delay investing in improvements to your store as long as possible. There's just no other way to make an existing chain deliver the numbers demanded by the Street on a quarterly basis.

You can't reformat a Kroger's to become a Whole Foods; it's more than wide aisles and abundance. Whole Foods started with its organic, ethical vision a slight 25 years ago and has been refining and improving upon it. Kroger's and Food Emporium and

A&P and IGA started with their visions too, and decades earlier, but the lines between those visions blurred years ago. By and large, we're left with a choice based on proximity, not on value, service, or quality that makes a shopper drive to ShopRite rather than a Grand Union. Each store is essentially the same. The only difference is the distance from your door.

Not so with Wegmans. According to shoppers with a Wegmans anywhere within driving range, it is well worth the trip and easy to bypass other stores along the route. So how does Wegmans do it? Just like Missy Park, the Wegman family is making long-term decisions to sustain a relationship with the shopper—not Wall Street analysts. It is a privately-held company. The chain treasures the foodiness of food itself. There is a celebration of it, within those aisles, that is joyous.

Indeed, each of the great food showcases I looked at—Whole Foods, FreshDirect, Wegmans—had an essential cheerfulness in common. The inherent, honest excitement of seasonality, a panorama of choices artfully arranged, signs that educate the palate rather than bark price, and an informed willing staff—all work together to create a *Shopportunity!* rather than an ordeal. An investment in fine living, rather than a fixed cost of weekly drudgery.

What happens to the rest? Grocery stores are at a crossroads—and enduring an identity crisis. Squeezed by Wal*Mart superstores and the club stores on the low price side of the equation, their finer wares are increasingly undermined by the emergence of upscale "food purveyors" who focus beautifully on high margin goods and make a terrific business out of it. Williams-Sonoma is one great example, with its Pumpkin Quick Bread, designer pasta sauces, esoteric salts and commitment to the construction of trophy cocktails. Citarella, Dean & Deluca, Zabar's and the return of Balducci's elate New Yorkers and online shoppers with alluring arrays of high-end options as well.

Even at the low-end, you need not go to a Wal*Mart superstore if there's a Trader Joe's in your area. The wit and wisdom of Trader Joe's is legendary. Its pathway through price is to create its own brands, rather than buying the packaged goods, beverages and products that arrive with a nationally advertised pedigree. Trader Joe's does its own take on nearly everything from seafood to coffee to breads to vitamins. Indeed the chain, which has 200 stores nationwide, boasts 80 percent of its inventory is made up of its own branded products, including the "Two-Buck Chuck" red wine that turned wine snobbism on its nose a couple of years ago. And, it explains, it pays its suppliers "in cash and on time," so that companies want to work with them. Sweet.

But where does a Kroger's, for example, go to grow? It's not going to turn itself into a Whole Foods or a Trader Joe's. It can't compete on the scale of Wal*Mart, nor will it ever make the investment in its people or its shoppers that a Wegmans does. Well, it's not going to be pretty. Next up from Kroger's is a new concept called, apparently, Food4Less, a no-frills warehouse. Augh. I'm not making this up. It appears that there will soon be just high-end and low-end grocery shopping with only a rapidly eroding group of regional chains stranded at the margins.

And so, on to Rule #14: Feed your mind: It's not just food. Seek knowledge. Rediscover discovery. Nurture your spirit. Not just through what you're buying, but in how you're buying, the experience itself should thrill the senses. If the guy behind the counter isn't interested in what you're buying from him, don't buy it. Go elsewhere.

Rule #14: Feed Your Mind

And Rule #15: Seek the Ethic. Just as you want to know who made your wine, who made your coat, who made your bread, figure out who is the puppeteer pulling the strings of your current grocery store. Shop the privately held, ideally family-run store, like Wegmans if you can. Or the one with an ethic you admire, like Whole Foods or Wild Oats. Maybe investigate the attitude of a Trader Joe's if you've got one of them near you. Perhaps, avoid the whole issue, if you're lucky enough to be in a FreshDirect neighborhood. Maybe move to Manhattan if you don't have one?

Rule #15: *Seek the Ethic*

Rule #16, Shop outside your culture. Seek new worlds in old worlds. Explore. Every so often, remember Laura. Move out of your usual shopping circuit and find a farmer's market or an ethnic neighborhood and shop there. Do something, make something, eat something you've never done, made, eaten before.

Rule #16: *Shop Old Worlds That Are New To You*

And now on to Wal*Mart. Dante said that the final ring of the Inferno would not be hot, but cold. Far from the heat or the light. I imagine it rather like a basic Wal*Mart store. Cold, calculating, inhuman and impervious: Abandon hope (of a *Shopportunity!*) all ye who enter here.

Ten

The Wal*Martization of the Universe: Must Its Value Trump Our Values?

There must have been something in the water supply in 1962. Somehow, three retailing giants were spawned nearly simultaneously. Wal*Mart, in Rogers, Arkansas. Target in Roseville, Minnesota. Kmart in Garden City, Michigan.

And thus the three major points on the discount compass were calibrated. Wal*Mart expanded throughout the Southeast. Target expanded from the Midwest. Kmart expanded throughout the Northeast. Today, all three are fully national. Wal*Mart is a huge global empire. The Dayton-Hudson Company is but a vague retail memory, rechristened in honor of Target's success. Kmart, spawn of the famed "five-and-dime" Kresge, has acquired the venerable Sears.

At this moment in this country there are 3,808 Wal*Marts of some sort (basic Wal*Mart stores, Supercenters, Sam's Clubs and Neighborhood Markets), 1,400 Target (basic and SuperTargets), 1,479 Kmarts (basic and Kmart Super Centers). Add to that 1,970 Sears stores, 346 Costco warehouses, and 160 or so BJs and that's 9,163 stores with a conservative average of 100,000 different items per store or 9,163 million things to buy at discount at any moment.

Each of these stores is on average about 100,000 square feet, which means 9,163 million square feet of our country devoted to discount shopping. Just for perspective, in 1970, we roamed about 11,011 shopping centers in this country. By 2004, it had grown to 47,718 such shopping areas, nearly all of them "anchored" by a Wal*Mart, Target, Kmart or Sears. What more could a consumer society want?

Yet studies show that we're spending roughly the same percentage of our income on general merchandise, apparel, furniture, consumer electronics, books and music: about 24 percent. So, if we're spending the same percentage of our incomes on stuff, and our incomes are rising all the while the stuff gets cheaper, where's all the stuff? What happens to it? Where does it go?

Lots of it is in the landfills, refusing to decay. A great portion is in storage locker facilities, a relatively recent industry, but one of the country's fastest growing. And some of it shows up on eBay, creating what is becoming the antithesis of "an ownership society." We simply buy it, use it, sell it—or toss it or store it. Little rises to the level of wedding dress in this world.

If the Procter & Gamble marketing thesis—respond to consumer needs with genuinely superior products and market them supremely well—still holds, then these behemoths of stuff have clearly tapped a rich vein of need and they have marketed themselves extremely well. It's the responding with "genuinely superior products" that trips me up, though. Sam Walton wrote in his autobiography that one of the keys to great retailing is to "exceed your customers' expectations." He wrote, "If you do, they'll come back over and over."

Does Wal*Mart today actually exceed our expectations? Or has it so lowered our hopes for the shopping experience that we simply want to get in and out? We figure all these stores are equally tough on customers and salespeople alike? Is the shopping experience in these cavernous stores really superior to my local hardware or clothing or housewares or consumer electronics stores?

And why is Wal*Mart the most spectacularly successful of the discount entities? What is it about the experience it provides that accounts for its breakout performance? Because you see, Wal*Mart and Exxon vie with each other for the top of *Fortune* magazine's list as the largest American company in the world.

Let's repeat that.

Wal*Mart competes with Exxon for the status of largest American company in the world.

Not General Motors, IBM, not General Electric, not Microsoft, not my beloved Procter & Gamble, not Kraft. Not any company you think of as being larger actually is larger than Wal*Mart. It employs more people than any other private sector company in the world.

And yet, its appeal eludes me.

"Of course it does," says Brett Stover, my global retailing expert. "When talking about Wal*Mart the first thing I have to remind people is the vast majority of folks you will be having this conversation with are not the Wal*Mart target shopper. But you need to remember: You are the minority."

Brett attributes Wal*Mart's remarkable success to five key factors: First, price, price, price. They own low price. Even when the shopper knows they might pay more for something at Wal*Mart than somewhere else, they rest assured that overall they pay less "basket for basket."

Second, Wal*Mart sits on top of the American archetype: red, white and blue. It epitomizes family values. It celebrates home. It pays homage to good old Sam who started with nothing and built one of the world's largest companies. "From Grandpa greeting you at the door to the American flags on the way out, it is America," explains Brett. "Everything about it screams Americana—and in the United States that's a good thing. Global expansion, of course, requires different ways to connect with consumers and that's why we have seen hit and miss as they have expanded globally."

Third, the sense of work and reward. Wal*Mart isn't about pretty. It's about long lines and putting in the effort to look for the deals. The reward is the savings and the hope that your friends and family perceive you as a "smart shopper," willing to sacrifice for your family. Shopping at Wal*Mart is "sensible" in this world view.

Fourth, the urge to scrimp in order to splurge. A great many of the items we shop for at a Wal*Mart are in the "okay, available and cheap" class of goods. We don't notice them until we run out and so we avoid the pitfall of being without diapers or toilet paper or tissues, but once we've scored the basics, we've saved enough to explore the "fun" items in the store. "Wal*Mart shoppers would feel guilty about buying these goods in a specialty store," says Brett. "But because they are not making a special trip and they've already done the serious shopping, they get to treat themselves with a new tool, or a new food product, or something pampering from the beauty care aisle."

And finally, It's a family place. The shopper can take the kids and the grandparents to Wal*Mart and everyone will find something to buy—and not anything offensive. Special edition videos and CDs are made for Wal*Mart shoppers to ensure it's family friendly. Important, because it's a big, noisy, messy place, shoppers feel okay about letting their kids have the run of the store. "Nobody has to be on 'best behavior' at Wal*Mart," Brett tells me. "It's real."

But, what if you're Target? Or Kmart? Or Sears? The moment the teeter-totter tottered the other way came as a little heralded, but nonetheless epoch shifting event: One day in 2000, the Dayton-Hudson Company changed its name. To Target. A respected department store chain just wasn't sexy or compelling enough to Wall Street, but a discount merchant was. Another moment came four years later as Kmart acquired Sears. Not enough room at the bottom for these two legendary retailers.

So, we have to stand back and just gaze at Wal*Mart, one of the two biggest American companies on the planet, the world's largest retailer, with nearly $300 billion in sales. The company employs 1.6 million associates worldwide through more than 3,700 facilities in the United States and more than 2,400 units in Argentina, Brazil, Canada, China, Costa Rica, El Salvador, Germany, Guatemala, Honduras, Japan, Mexico, Nicaragua, Puerto Rico, South Korea and the United Kingdom. More than 138 million customers per week visit Wal*Mart stores worldwide.

According to *Forbes* magazine Wal*Mart operates in 44 countries and has more than 100,000 associates in Mexico alone. According to *Retail Forward,* the company will top $500 billion by 2010. To what effect? "Good-bye mom-and-and-pop stores, good-bye local stores in local places," writes Robert Malone in *Forbes.*

Clearly there is a tremendous appeal. And there is tremendous cause for concern. First, let's consider the appeal. Sam was the stuff of legend. An American original. A real life Horatio Alger. Sam did the hula on Wall Street at high noon, making good on a promise he'd made to associates that he'd do it if the company achieved 8 percent pretax profit. What a guy! Sam started with a passion to make life affordable to everyday people and, by and large, he succeeded beyond anyone's wildest imaginings. He made a fabulous fortune for himself, his family and for many thousands of his colleagues. Tough not to respect his achievements.

So is Wal*Mart simply the celebration of an American success story, the legend of a visionary man named Sam who set out to sell the things people needed at a price they could afford? Is it a tale of a man who built a better mousetrap and the world has trod a well-worn path to his door in Bentonville, Arkansas? Is it the saga of a man who created jobs and careers for employees, while having a happy little yellow ball bounce around his stores, chainsaw in hand, slashing prices for the good of all?

Well, if you rely on Wal*Mart commercials, attend its annual meetings, or pay attention when its executives are interviewed on television, it is the American Dream come true. Absolutely. A man. A plan. A mission. A vision.

We see the happy yellow ball bouncing around—the chainsaw is a bit off-putting, but metaphorically accurate. We hear the happy stories of enthusiastic employees. We see the current chief executive officer of Wal*Mart, Lee Scott, earnestly telling an interviewer that when he comes to New York he shares a room with a business colleague and pays $10 for dinner, because he wants to make sure he's saving the company's money. We hear a corporate communications executive describing how hard the company works to make sure that the third-world factories are managed at the very highest standards.

The genius of Wal*Mart, according to another colleague who preferred to speak off the record because—as the head of a major consumer products company—his bread and butter, so to speak, is Wal*Mart, told me there are five touch points to consider. Just as Brett Stover had boiled down the success to five elements of consumer insights, so has this executive, albeit a different five, based on his understanding of the retailer on the business of its business.

First, Wal*Mart is an "extreme learning culture." This is code, he explains, for "they steal well and from anywhere." If something works for another retailer, Wal*Mart will rip it off and make it work for them.

Next, Sam was brilliant early on. He chose his battles wisely.

"They picked the right markets, the markets that nobody else wanted. They started in the Southeast and stayed there for more than a decade, then they learned and grew from there," my colleague tells me. He's also the one who says that when he looks at a map of Wal*Mart's expansion through time and the development of America's obesity epidemic over the same period, he believes it's a perfect correlation: In comes cheap food in big quantities and up go our scale numbers and waistline measurements.

Third, "Wal*Mart is obsessive about carving costs out of the system." Logistics, logistics, logistics. Theirs and their suppliers. They've literally changed the way everyone who deals with them does business, showing them how to shave tenths, hundredths, even thousandths of a cent out of manufacturing or shipping processes.

Fourth, they bring to it an "Arkansas underdog" quality. This exec explains that while you'd expect a huge company to get bigger under a Republican administration, as indeed it has, in its radical growth period in the 1990s, a fellow Arkansas native in the White House looked the other way when a more conventional Democrat's position might have demanded a consideration of issues of monopoly.

And, finally, there was from the earliest days almost a pyramid scheme of employee ownership through stock purchase, he recalls. The dream was kept alive for Wal*Mart employees that if they worked hard and well they could own a piece of the action. That made for powerful loyalty, and a willingness to cut certain corners that helped the company deliver on its "We Sell for Less" pledge.

But, there is life, indeed, reality beyond commercials, beyond Websites, beyond press releases. This is where, for me, the causes of tremendous appeal begin to collide with the causes of tremendous concern. Perhaps not all is rosy through Wal*Mart's tinted glasses.

I searched out Ian Rattray, again, this time to ask him about

Wal*Mart's success. Ian's been around long enough to have heard the stories firsthand from guys who traveled with Sam, how they'd go into a market and look at the small-town stores. "They'd first look at the pharmacies, then the hardware stores and then the photography shops," he told me.

"They'd analyze those and decide how best to take their employees and their customers. Yes, I've heard they'd place bets on how long it would take before these small mom-and-pop stores would be driven out of business. It was a game they knew they'd win, the only question was when. They'd bet on the exact date each one would fall. They were cocky about it." Indeed, nearly everyone I spoke to confided a certain "arrogance" in Wal*Mart's attitude to its vendors, if not "holier than thou," certainly "knowier than thou."

This is where the drumming of troubling stories begins to beat louder. The press coverage has been particularly vigilant lately, so we're getting to know another side to the legend. There are the stories of Wal*Mart subcontracting store cleanup to firms that lock the crews inside the stores at night. There are the stories of Wal*Mart employees expected to work "off the clock," which means that although they will be paid for an eight-hour shift, they will actually work an extra half hour or hour to get the job done the Wal*Mart way. There are the stories of Wal*Mart's blanket refusal to allow its associates to unionize. Remember too, the famed Kathy Lee Gifford "sweat shop" clothing brouhaha? It continues up to today's headlines, deconstructing the $14 toy at Wal*Mart that costs the Chinese manufacturer 18 cents to make, because of the working conditions of its employees.

As Wal*Mart moves out of its rural and suburban comfort zone and tries to crack into the big leagues of major American cities, such as Los Angeles, Chicago and New York, the welcome mat has been withdrawn. There have been some high profile defeats for the company as it attempts to move into these markets.

Indeed, a McKinsey & Company study for Wal*Mart "found that 2 percent to 8 percent of Wal*Mart consumers surveyed have ceased shopping at the chain because of 'negative press they have heard.' " Another McKinsey study also discussed the company's health-care policy. The Wal*Mart Website describes its health-care plans as being developed to help employees in catastrophic situations, which is, of course, the least expensive and least used benefit. McKinsey told the company that perhaps it should consider improving the coverage, but also hiring only those employees least likely to need it—those in good health. It suggested making picking up shopping carts from the parking lot an essential aspect of every cashier's job, so that only those able to do this kind of work (think about walking those massive parking lots, pushing a dozen or so carts) need apply.

The hope of a significant turnaround in Wal*Mart's core vision is bleak. A jury ruled that Wal*Mart must pay $172 million over meal breaks it systematically denied its associates. The last paragraph of the article quotes a Wal*Mart spokesperson and continues to amaze: "Wal*Mart has since taken steps to ensure all associates receive their meal periods, including adopting new technology that sends alerts to cashiers when it is time for their meal breaks. The system will automatically shut down registers if the cashier does not respond."

The implication, of course, is clear: Those pesky cashiers got us in all this trouble by not taking their meal breaks. Well, our technology will outsmart them. Associates take note: no more skipping meals.

Lawmakers in 30 states are following the lead of Maryland, which has enacted legislation that affects only Wal*Mart, demanding companies that employ more than 10,000 people in the state must provide affordable health care. These attempts to get Wal*Mart to meet some sort of minimum standard are the direct result of the company's approach to benefits: adding thousands to the rolls of state-sponsored programs, rather than providing affordable health care to its employees.

And why can't Wal*Mart pay a living wage and provide affordable health care to its employees? John Tierney, op-ed columnist for the *New York Times,* says it's the difference between a Wal*Mart and a Costco: Costco in his mind "needs to pay [better wages] because it requires higher-skilled workers to sell higher-end products to its more affluent customers."

Roberta Rosenberger, writing to the paper, says, "Excuse me? Costco is a warehouse! There is very little in the way of one-on-one shopping help. The last time I shopped at Costco, there was no one to help me distinguish between a Sony computer and a Hewlett-Packard. But there were lots of forklift operators, butchers, pharmacists, cash-register clerks and a slew of retirement-aged men and women giving out samples of food. Is it this last group that Mr. Tierney considers 'higher skilled'? Wal*Mart pays its full-time employees $9.68 an hour on average. Last year, it paid its chief executive $17.5 million in total compensation, about twice the average pay of leading American chief executives. The company made a profit of $10.3 billion."

The salary of the chief of Costco? Capped by corporate fiat: a salary of 15 times the lowest-paid worker, or about $350,000 last year, plus bonus. Now we don't have to take up a collection for him, there are stock options, but it does show—along with Costco's higher wages to employees, willingness to unionize, agreement to pay graciously for health care—that there are sound, credible business practices that allow discount retailers to provide shoppers with value, while valuing their employees.

Beyond the pervasive impact that Wal*Mart has on the everyday lives of us all, it is also exporting its culture. Wal*Mart ranks as China's sixth largest export market, right behind Germany. It bought some $18 billion worth of goods from the Chinese in 2004 alone. Wal*Mart, with its bottom-line–driven pricing and logistics expertise, is educating the Chinese manufacturing community, there's no doubt about that. According to Alejandra Domenzain, associate director of Sweatshop Watch, "Wal*Mart is both a beneficiary and a driver of the race to the bottom in the global economy," she told *Time* magazine. "It has enormous leverage, and how it uses that leverage in the pursuit of ever-cheaper labor has enormous consequences for communities in the United States."

This relentless pressure on price kind of sits comfortably with Lee Scott's homey discussions of executives flying coach, sharing hotel rooms and eating dinner on the cheap. But, well, gosh, Lee made somewhere between $17 million and $27 million last year (depending upon who you talk to), so it seems an artificial, even bizarre economy on his part at best.

And, of course, there is the flat-out assumption that low price trumps any sense of community that might linger in this country. Consider the Wal*Mart factor as it plays out in the American textile industry. Steve Dobbins is president and CEO of Carolina Mills, supplying thread, yarn and textile finishing to apparel makers. As manufacturing heads offshore, the likelihood of a company's buying American wares declines day after day. "People ask, 'How can it be bad for things to come into the United States cheaply? How can it be bad to have a bargain at Wal*Mart?' Sure, it's held inflation down and it's great to have bargains, but you can't buy anything if you're not employed. We are shopping ourselves out of jobs."

We may well be shopping ourselves out of jobs. And into obesity, of course. And we're driving little companies to the mat for no good reason, other than we'd like to pay a little bit less for something—indeed, for every little thing—in order to feel, what? that we're sensible shoppers? That we've gotten one over on the system? Why are we able to look the other way and imagine that the cashier who gamely dons a Santa hat and wishes us "Happy

Holidays" at Christmas should be happy to make minimum wage and work two jobs so that we can save $6.59 on our groceries?

Americans already spend less on food as a percentage of our income than citizens of most industrialized nations and all developing economies. Our food is cheap enough. Indeed, it's probably too cheap for our own good already.

Adam Hanft, a columnist for *Fast Company* and also the chief executive officer of Hanft Unlimited, had other advice for Wal*Mart. Writing in Fast Company.com he suggested a 10-step plan, including firing its consultants (bunker mentality types), canceling the celebrity-infested commercials (not credible), and talking to the unions (respectful). Most appealingly, Adam asks Wal*Mart to apply its fabled price-cutting skills to HMOs and prescription pharmaceuticals in order to provide employees with real and affordable health-care and wellness benefits.

Let's see if the company does anything differently.

It has about three options, as far as I can tell: Wal*Mart can pull up the bridges around the moat and just deny, deny, deny that it's ever done anything wrong and continue to pay multimillion-dollar fines to various states on various charges as they appear. Wal*Mart can do a McDonald's and reorient itself: Look at how the fortunes of that one-time poster child of poor nutrition have improved by just adding salads to the menu, switching from the trans fat it fried its fries in, and putting Ronald on a diet and exercise regimen. (Although the sales growth fueling its turnaround comes at the expense of those able only to afford to order from its $1 menu.) Wal*Mart can change the subject and start doing something right in an entirely different sphere than employee compensation and benefits.

My off-the-record colleague tells me they are serious about changing the subject: Wal*Mart will now address the environmental impact of all this stuff. It will make organic farming products affordable to the mainstream. It will get serious about reducing, reusing and recycling the waste its merchandise contributes to our landfills.

They will, he tells me too, begin ultimately to learn how to face up to societal issues. They just haven't had to before, because they never tried to compete in high profile markets with high stakes public policy scrutiny. We'll see. This is an open experiment too: How does Wal*Mart use its "learning culture" to adapt to metrics beyond the financial statement? It will be fascinating to watch.

Wal*Mart, which accounts for 10 percent of retail sales in this country, was a drag on the market Christmas 2005. Its strategy of going with deep discounts early did not appear to sustain it through the season. And, important for the hope for a return to "the thrill of the hunt" in our shopping experience, the big winners were Target, Neiman-Marcus, Nordstrom, Saks and Abercrombie & Fitch, each of whom brings value beyond low price to the equation.

So I take myself to a Wal*Mart to see reality firsthand. It is every bit as chaotic and messy as Brett has described it. The parking lot is filled with a cross section of late model shiny Lexus SUVs and patchwork painted cars that make weird noises while idling outside. Was that a drug deal going down in the parking lot or just two friends hanging? Once I'd parked, I looked about to see where exactly I was, so I could find my way back, but no clearly marked signs showed me the way. Every light stanchion bore the notice that Security Cameras Are In Use. It was broad daylight, but more than a little scary. Large signs at the entrance clearly make Wal*Mart's point: We Sell For Less. Even the vending machines of Coke and bottled water delivered the benefit: $1 cans and bottles.

The vague but euphoric greeters I'd remembered from my last visit perhaps a decade before seemed, well, less euphoric to be saying "Welcome to Wal*Mart." The wheels squeaked irritatingly on my cart. The first sight to really dwell on was the Customer Service station near the entrance: A line of people returning merchandise snaked its way around the front of the store, customers waiting to lodge their complaints to the lone service person on duty. "Satisfaction Guaranteed," yes, of course. But satisfaction delayed.

The Family Fun Center also near the front of the store was silent, bereft of the cacophony of kids, perhaps because the bulletin board at the entrance had been given over to photos of missing children. Hard to imagine leaving your child alone in such a place after passing by that terrifying montage.

The Wal*Mart TV Network blared from plasma screen TV sets throughout the store. Deals, sales, cheery news of new price cuts chipperly drowned out the sound of my squeaking cart. Through the din the public address system broke through: "Register Trained Associate to Check Out!" What must it mean to be "register trained"? The mix of languages being spoken in the aisles conjured an imagined sound track of Ellis Island's immigration depot, circa 1900.

Wal*Mart is a loud, boisterous, difficult place to shop. Its Action Alley along the perimeter, where all the advertised and unadvertised specials vie for shopper attention, seems like a carnival barker's dream come true. So much stuff. And still there is room in the cart. And all so cheap. We have to buy more.

But the essential sadness of the in-store experience haunts. The mindless pushing of the carts, the arguing parents in the aisles, the Wal*Mart shopper's uniform—jeans, athlete shoes and sweatshirts with weird, self-deprecating messages, including I'm Out of My Mind, Try Back Tomorrow and Aren't You Glad I'm Not a Twin—don't auger the vision of populist delight in value, convenience and service.

So Wal*Mart, the 600-pound gorilla of retailing, has some decisions to make. Let's hope they return to Sam's notion of respecting associates and customers alike—and the merchandise, too. A couple of tough quarters and a dustup in the pages of our newspapers and magazines may well kick this "learning culture" into gear—and get it to clean up the stores and its act.

I first saw the blip of Wal*Mart on my radar screen about 20 years ago. I was walking through the corridors at Procter & Gamble and I heard hoots, hollers, and the general hilarity of a celebration coming from one of the cubicles. It was someone who worked on the Crest brand hosting a spontaneous party because he'd just received a copy of the new Wal*Mart circular offering Crest at 99 cents a tube.

I could not understand what the euphoria was about, because—in my naïveté—I thought that selling Crest for less was denigrating to the brand. But no. Not in this model. Just as Diane needs to keep the Andrew Marc manufacturing lines running year round, Crest wanted to move a lot of goods through its factories. And, at 99 cents, there were sure to be shoppers picking Crest rather than Colgate. Wal*Mart was using the Crest price as a "loss-leader," which simply means they were offering it at a price that would bring people to the store—and once there, they'd buy much more.

I was at P&G that day to present to the Crest brand group my thoughts, among them that Crest had tremendous consumer permission to move beyond toothpaste and into other oral-care products. I was pretty much booed out of the room. The brand manager lectured me that Crest would always be a toothpaste. "Crest!" he screamed at me when I suggested going into toothbrushes and mouthwash. "Crest will always be a toothpaste! It will always have a red *C* and dark blue *R,* and light blue *E* . . ." Well, you get the drift. Not a high point in my career.

About a decade later, P&G was worried. The balance had shifted and rather than Wal*Mart using discounted Crest to bring shoppers in, it was telling Procter how to make its product more efficiently, the price at which Wal*Mart would be willing to buy it and the price that it would be selling its own store brand. That price gap was pennies per tube. P&G, in Wal*Mart's view, could just suck it up.

Studies over the years had shown that every packaged goods category can have three tiers of products: Branded and marketed toothpastes, like Crest, Colgate and AquaFresh; midrange products, such as Ipana, Gleem, Arm & Hammer; and store brands, typically lower quality to justify the lower price. Suddenly, upstarts like Rembrandt were beginning to create a superpremium level, Crest was being pushed into the midrange and Ipana and Gleem were going the way of the buggy whip. Sam's American Choice brands were putting pressure on Procter & Gamble by owning the bottom shelf and providing a pretty good product into the bargain. Wal*Mart set the "floor" pricing, Rembrandt set the top—and P&G's Crest was being caught in the middle.

A Bain & Company consulting study was published saying that any company with more than 30 percent of its sales moving through Wal*Mart was in deep trouble. But it didn't take an authoritative report to make that point. All you had to do was walk the halls of any major packaged goods or food company. The hand-wringing was at an all-time high. Wal*Mart was dictating the terms of their business model: If Wal*Mart was happy with a 2 percent profit on sales, then why shouldn't P&G's shareholders be too?

Well, they weren't. Procter & Gamble went through a freefall in 2000. Stock price tumbled, corporate ranks were downsized, its retirees' pension funds eroded out from under them, all to be able to deal with Wal*Mart on Wal*Mart's terms. And P&G was not alone in its worry. At Jiffy Lube, there was concern that Wal*Mart was getting into the quick-lube business. At Levi's the debate raged whether or not to start selling its goods at Wal*Mart, which they ultimately decided to do. A great many urgent meetings took place in every office park and corporate campus in the land.

P&G took a deep breath and began to reinvent Crest (and other of its brands) to insulate them from promotions based purely on price—and particularly Wal*Mart's everyday low price demands. Well, they've done it—and the Crest logo comes in a variety of colors too. They've expanded into toothbrushes, both manual and battery-powered, they've pioneered the commercializing of home tooth-whitening systems, and they've put Scope (another P&G product) in some versions of the product.

Working hard to create and maintain a direct relationship with consumers, they created the Crest Dental Plan online. And, modeled on that, they created the Tide Fabric Care Network, which puts their incredible knowledge about stain removal and clothing care to good advantage.

They had the discipline to get out of all food products, except the multibillion-dollar Pringles brand. And they invested heavily in new categories of products, like Swiffer, the floor cleaning system, Febreze, the fabric odor cleansing system, and Dryel, the in-home dry-cleaning system. Note the move to "systems," rather than mere products or brands.

In short, they've done what P&G is best at, innovation upon innovation, coming so fast that even Wal*Mart can't keep up, and, thereby protecting their brands from "okay, available and cheap" status.

Peter Klein, the strategy maven who's shadowed Jim Kilts for a big part of Kilts's career—at General Foods, Kraft Foods, Nabisco and then at Gillette—tells me this system approach has been a big winner for both P&G and Gillette, which was acquired by P&G in 2005. "The thing we've seen time after time is the power of creating a business platform with specific retailers from which you can move the consumer up the chain," he tells me. "In toothbrushes, you move up from manual to rechargeable. In batteries too, you move from basic to rechargeable. In shaving, we go from disposables to a shaving system to a super premium razor, like Mach3 or Fusion. We're constantly innovating on the super-premium business."

Many people looking at P&G's acquisition of Gillette thought the Wal*Mart defense strategy was showing a bit. The move looked calculated to give P&G much more negotiating clout by bringing both its current female-centric brands and now alpha male Gillette brands to the table. Could Wal*Mart really do without these brands? If not, then it has lost some of its "like it or lump it" advantage when mandating prices to P&G.

But what if you're not P&G? What if you're Vlasic? Well, we know that sad story. What if you're Lion Brand Yarns? David Blumenthal is the president and CEO of Lion Brand Yarn Company. He's the fourth generation of his family to run the company and he's hoping to pass it along to the next generation.

On his watch, the company has grown to nearly $200 million in sales, thanks in large part to his embracing the need to lead the knitting and crocheting industry, creating a Website (www.lion brand.com), copublishing his own magazines with *Better Homes & Gardens, Vogue Knitting* and *Woman's Day,* even capitalizing on the celebrity culture to showcase famous knitters, including Vanna White for the past 12 years, and publicizing the Lion Brand pattern that created the cell-block poncho made famous as Martha Stewart's parting gift from her one-time neighbors. With more than 1.8 million downloads for that single pattern, he's surely struck a resonant chord with America's knitters.

Today, this little-company-that-could stands at a crossroads. The category is big enough that Wal*Mart has noticed it. And what Wal*Mart notices, it wants to make cheaper. Poof! Why bother with Lion Brand Yarn, when Wal*Mart can go to his suppliers around the globe and buy directly? David is in Procter & Gamble's position of a decade ago—without the clout and wherewithal P&G could bring to the party. What's the company to do?

I'd like us just to watch Lion Brand Yarns over the next couple of years and see how it rises to the occasion, or simply cannot compete with the race to the bottom mentality we seem not only to embrace as a nation, but also to be exporting. This is a genuine real-time experiment to see if a fourth generation company can sustain itself and even grow in the face of price, price, price pressure. Are there values beyond value that we're willing to pay for?

David is optimistic. He tells me that he believes retailers who have attempted to create their own private label yarns are finding disappointing results. "It's more than price for a real knitter," he explains. "It's the quality, the color palette, texture, it's the patterns, it's the help and advice. Knitters know what they're doing and they rely on trusted brands like ours to help create their projects successfully. This really isn't a commodity business. It's a creative endeavor."

He makes excellent sense, I think. Time will tell.

And what of those other members of the triplets, born at the same time, but certainly not identical. What of Target, or as it is termed Targée by teens and hip urbanites who want to grant themselves permission to shop at a discount merchant? What of Kmart?

The people at Target seem to have decided not to underestimate the taste of the American shopper. Everything from the Michael Graves teapots and other kitchenwares to the clean, elegant store design to the wit of its advertising suggests that money isn't the only thing shoppers value.

Target delivers a broad and even eclectic range of products, as I witnessed firsthand with Mattie, searching simultaneously for a belt to help hold up her new jeans one day—and a can of her favorite chips, Pringles. Both under one roof, clearly marked, plus courteous service and clean restrooms into the bargain. We'd actually gone through a small-town shopping area, plus an entire mall to find a little girl's belt and found it only at Target, wonderfully in pink.

And given a bit of breathing room on price, the company is able to pay better wages, be somewhat more rigorous about its factory conditions and have a far more comprehensive benefits package than Wal*Mart's. It attracts fashion designers like Isaac Mizrahi, Fiorucci, and Mossimo to bring to life its "Expect More. Pay Less" pledge. In fact, after renaming itself Target, it appears to have leveraged that old Dayton-Hudson retail heritage smartly by using its contacts and expertise to bring a genuinely exciting fashion sensibility to its customers.

I tremble for Kmart, though. Several years ago I did some work for the company, when it was imperiously housed in a fortresslike Darth Vader building in Troy, Michigan. The place seemed designed to make you feel small and insignificant. Probably all the better to help Kmart negotiate with vendors, but still. Off-putting. The company has fallen on hard times, because it lost its way. Wal*Mart stands for price. Target stands for accessible design. But, Kmart? Well, it just seems cheap, Martha Stewart notwithstanding. On my visits to Kmart, the cashiers are standing at attention at the front of their stations, like privates awaiting inspection, but alas! to no point, few customers dot the aisles, fewer still push to edge out their fellows at the checkout.

Its purchase of Sears will doubtless give Kmart economies of scale, but what is Sears but a roof over the head of Kenmore appliances and Craftsman tools? Who would go there without these stalwart brands? I'm just not sure. These are quickly becoming real estate companies, more vital for the land and buildings than for their wares.

Beyond these basic discount chains, there are the club stores: Sam's Clubs; Costco, and BJs. When I interview women about their shopping experiences in these massive warehouse stores for which they pay a membership fee to enter, they really do describe the adventure as a "treasure hunt," something akin to a trip to Las Vegas.

If Wal*Mart is about getting the basics sensibly and then splurging on something fun, then the club stores are about a journey into the unknown. As one interviewee explained it, "Sometimes my girlfriends and I go to Las Vegas for a weekend. A trip to a Costco is just like that. We go together. We split the cost. We never know what we're going to find. We're going to spend more than we planned. When we go to check out we're never sure our credit cards will clear. And when we get home, we realize the gallon jar of mayonnaise doesn't fit in the refrigerator. We feel a little bit angry at ourselves, but excited for the next time."

I have to confess that when Mattie was still in diapers and I was living in East Hampton, my worst fear was running out of diapers in the middle of the night. So whenever I went back and forth to the city, I would consider a stop off at Sam's Club, visible from the Long Island Expressway. I've never felt more like a single mother than I did walking through those overpowering aisles, dwarfed by towering forests of things. I'd get disoriented easily and I must have bought enough Cascade to last a lifetime, because I could never remember if I had bought it the last time or not.

If the first time I went it was just for large boxes of diapers, little by little I got to know the store a bit, got used to the size of the wagons, became inured to the scale and the vertigo of going from computers to industrial-size Reynolds Wrap in the space of a few feet. Pretty soon, I realized I needed a freezer in the basement in order to allow me to take advantage of the food for sale, the frozen hors d'oeuvres, the filets, the mini pizzas. Now, clearly, I wasn't thinking rationally, because how much would I have had to buy (for a family of two) in order to save enough to pay for a freezer, but buy a freezer I did.

There was something comforting about knowing that no matter what else happened, we'd never run out of diapers—or pastry shells. I chalk part of it up to the anxiety of being a new mother and worrying about everything, and I have to say it wasn't the cheapness that called me, as much as the guarantee of not being alone in a house in the northwest woods of East Hampton with a child in need of a diaper. Still, I sensed the adventure there. Who knew what I'd find each time? In the midst of all the families pushing two carts and arguing with their children about what could and could not be bought this trip, there was a sense that I was doing something important and nurturing for my wee family.

Once I moved into the city again, of course, such luxuries as cases of Bounty in the basement became impossible, unless I wanted to rent a storage space 12 blocks away for all my backup goods. I had another savings busting idea (like a freezer), but this time I managed to "just say no." The club stores are definitely a suburban phenomenon. Urban dwellers have no room to store the loot.

I know from my own experience and from interviews with scores of shoppers that this kind of shopping isn't just about price. There's a real quest going on, the search for the new and engaging, as well as a hope for safety, abundance and plenty. Of never running out. A powerful new definition of convenience—only shopping once a month.

But, hey! What about just going to a local butcher, toy store, photo shop or hardware store? If shopping were fun again, why would we want to only do it once a month? If clerks were paid a living wage, might they not look us in the eye and say, "I see you're buying chicken. Here's a great recipe." There are still stores and clerks like this, nearby shoe stores, local bakers, neighborhood candlestick makers.

In East Hampton, it was to the ladies of Round Swamp Farm I always turned when I wanted the best fruits, vegetables, fish, cookies or cinnamon rolls that rivaled my mother's. In New York, it is to the Greenwich Farmer's Market on Saturday mornings I stroll when I need jellies and jams. I may pay more than I would have at Sam's Club, but I buy fewer, better things. The food budget hasn't changed; in fact, it's less than when I was pantry loading on the Long Island Expressway.

What about starting with your very next purchase to breathe life back into our small towns and city centers? What about beginning to repeal the essential law of narcissism that these retailers rely upon: Who cares what happens to anyone else? I'm in it for myself. Cheaper is better, right? Well, maybe not.

So, Rule #17: Get out of the Big Box. It just couldn't be clearer. Shop with human beings who live in and care about your town and schools. Be part of your community. Shop the little guy.

Rule #17: Break Out of the Big Box

Let's drive on.

Eleven

On the Road Again: Convenience Stores, Gas Stations, Oil Changes and Dealerships

The day I first fell under the spell of Ian Rattray, my retail design guru and friend, was when I heard him explain the evolution of the convenience store and how it was really embedded in the ongoing transformation of the automotive industry itself. It seems that somewhere in the early 2000s there was a "tipping point" moment: These little stores adjacent to the gas pumps started pumping more profits than the pumps. Gas had become a price-sensitive commodity—what's the difference between Exxon Mobil's fuel and Texaco's? Shell's versus BP's? Is it a difference you're willing to drive out of your way to gain? Unlikely. A nickel a gallon difference in price might get your attention, but not one superior performance claim versus another. We just assume it's all pretty good, pretty much the same and pretty damn expensive to fill up.

All of a sudden this industry best known as having cornered the world's supply of Slim-Jims, Beer Nuts, slushy fruit drinks and bad coffee began to rouse itself.

"We'd come in to take a look at these stores and it was all so obvious," Ian explained. "There was bulletproof glass around the cashier and it faced the wrong way. We wanted women to come into these places and yet they were being told in the most direct way possible that it wasn't safe. Even the cashier was scared to be in there without protection."

The gas companies, in tandem with the franchise owners of the various stations—Exxon-Mobil, BP, Texaco, Phillips 66, Shell—everyone knew that the key to growing this part of their business simply required putting more goods in the store that women wanted, and getting more women to come into the stores. Men were going to buy the Slim Jims. Women would—if properly entreated and treated—buy tonight's family dinner. And, by and large, the story of the evolution of the automotive category is one of coming to terms with Sigmund Freud's famous question, "What do women want?"

Faith Popcorn, in her book *EVEolution,* stated the answer succinctly: "Men want a transaction. Women want a relationship." The difference between a one-night stand and a relationship, indeed, a marriage, for better or worse. Get a woman married to your store, forge a "dynamic connectedness," in Ian's parlance, and she'll forgive you for the occasional transgression. But how to get her married to a store she was reasonably enough afraid to enter?

Putting more stuff into the store was relatively easy, all about design, building and expanding. But the second part, getting her to believe she was wanted proved to be much, much harder. Nobody wanted to clean the restrooms for her, after all.

I remember a particularly garish example, right at the turnoff of Exit 70 of the Long Island Expressway as I'd leave the highway and begin the final part of the 100-mile trek to East Hampton. It was a Mobil station at the time, and after an hour or so on the road from Manhattan on a Friday night, it should have been a welcoming respite. Time to stretch your legs, use the facilities, buy some coffee or a snack, fill up the car and drive on. One visit to the restroom was all it took to convince me that I was not welcome there. I've been in cleaner outhouses at a summer music camp as a kid.

Beyond that, of course, there was that bulletproof glass protecting the cashier. There was that signature smell of burnt coffee in Pyrex pots, sizzling on the burners. It was, as Ian puts it, a "drop dead" communication direct from the store to me.

But that was then. This world is much different now. They've moved the outhouse in-house. Where once you had to beg the guy for a key to go back outside and around the corner of a darkened lot to use the unisex restroom, now there are relatively clean, seemingly sanitary men's and women's rooms obvious from the entryway. The aisles go off at angles at the doorways, beckoning us through to check out the wares. Logs in winter, coolers of beer and colas in summer, and best of all, really remarkable coffee bars.

The basic premise has stayed the same: Quick in and quicker out. But the fundamentals—milk, beer, cola, coffee, eggs, bacon, orange juice, white bread, ice, chips—are coupled with some realistically priced "nice to haves," like cake mixes, Rose's lime juice and peanut butter. The old wisdom was to price-gouge panic-stricken shoppers, desperately seeking tampons, disposable diapers or toilet paper at midnight. The new wisdom is a mini grocery store with fairly priced goods, cigarettes, coffee, plus lots and lots of lottery tickets.

According to Ian, there are four corners in the successful convenience map. First, the place: It must be convenient, both in hours it's open and its location. We judge this by seeing that it's clean and bright. Second, the people: polite and motivated, able to be energized and animated when dealing with customers and seeming to be trustworthy. Third, the company's principles must be clear. We want to know that they treat customers and employees with respect. We want it to have a reputation for integrity. And finally, the processes: We want to experience ourselves saving time; we want each interaction to be fast and accurate.

What happens over time when these four promises are delivered? Customers come in more often, buy more each time and learn to trust new offerings. Women, as it turns out, don't want a "one-night stand" from their stores or their cars: They want a relationship. They actually come to know the store, appreciate the value and become at first simply loyal to it, and ultimately advocates for it. The well-tuned convenience store delivers a "dynamic connectedness" that makes it a trusted, reliable resource as we negotiate the needs and demands of the everyday.

A woman driving home from work can fill up her car with gas while grabbing ingredients for a basic frozen-food dinner, ice cream bars for dessert, milk and cereal for tomorrow and be on her way, without paying a steep premium for the convenience. A guy on his way to work can grab cigarettes, a newspaper, a pretty fresh doughnut and a decent cup of coffee and be on the road again.

This remarkable shift did not happen in a vacuum. Gas station owners, whether the oil companies themselves or the franchisees, didn't wake up one morning and say, "Gosh, we'd better clean the restrooms, stock Nutri-Grain bars, and put lights in the parking lots, because we can't make money on gas and women don't trust us." In fact, it's a pretty tangled web to unweave. It shines a bright light on all of automotive.

Let's follow the money. The stations weren't making money at the pump and they were watching their service and maintenance business slowly erode, too. Remember the days when that local gas station really had bays set up for mechanics to work on cars?

Have you noticed there's not much of that going on? Well, there are a bunch of factors. One has been the increasingly complex technology under the hoods of our cars. It may have started with the European imports, but the pervasive complexity of today's cars means it really does take a rocket scientist to maintain them.

The intricacies of the engines demand factory authorized mechanics. The basics, such as noisy mufflers, oil changes and new tires, moved to price-touting specialists. Think Jiffy Lube, Tire City, and Midas Mufflers—"You're not going to pay a lot for that muffler!"

At BrainReserve in the late 1990s, Jim Postl, then president and CEO of Pennzoil/Quaker State, now owned by Shell, called us in to work on Jiffy Lube. The division was made up of company-owned and also franchised stores. The basic premise was that for a fixed fee, you'd get your oil changed and your oil filter replaced in ten minutes or so. They'd also visually inspect a number of potential issues: antifreeze and coolant reservoir levels, the engine air filtration system, the serpentine belts, the brake fluid level, wiper blades and exterior lights. They'd vacuum the floors, clean the exterior windows and check the tire pressure. They'd even top off other fluids, like transmission, power steering, windshield washer and battery water. In short a good deal, done inexpensively and fast. Should have been a sure thing, right?

Well, except for one thing. Real men change their own oil. Which meant that women were their primary customers, and women didn't really like the way Jiffy Lube went about these chores. In order to get it done fast, Jiffy Lube had developed a checklist and a system whereby one mechanic would come over to the driver's side of the car as the woman drove up. He'd swing open the door, ask her to get out quickly and take her child with her. Then the guys would start yelling at one another to ensure that they were doing everything on the list—yelling at one another and trying to move at warp speed.

This was, of course, a wildly upsetting scenario for the customer, more often than not more scared by the process than reassured. She and her child would be shunted into a tweedy "waiting room"—with that burned-coffee-in-the-Pyrex smell, a television set whose remote had been lost years ago and something worrisome on the carpeting. Jiffy Lube couldn't figure out why even as they got faster and faster at doing the job, women were less and less likely to go there.

It was rather like Tim Dimello's Streamline thinking: The chore is onerous, let's get it over with quickly. What BrainReserve found was that the speed wasn't the issue for women. And neither really was a dollar more or less. What they wanted was a place to wait that was welcoming for them and their children and a sense that the mechanics knew what they were doing. All the shouting and racing around didn't help anything.

The reality is women feel about those waiting rooms the way men feel about going to a lingerie shop to buy a negligee for their wives. They do want out fast. They feel how very much they don't belong here. So it was kind of logical that Jiffy Lube had concentrated on shortening the process, rather than making it more pleasurable. But by its unrelenting focus on speed and efficiency, the place was becoming increasingly inhospitable, as if the lingerie saleswomen started shouting out to one another, "Hey! he wants a 36B and a black leather thong!" "Got it! Check!" "Does he want a pair of fishnets?" "How about black stilettos?" "Hey! Tell him we've got a special on red leather bustiers today, too."

The first step was to redesign the waiting area, creating a nook for kids to safely play, putting in working television sets tuned to child-friendly channels and expanding the offerings for sale to include good coffee, snacks and magazines. Then, the mechanics had to be untaught the whole shouting ritual, reeducated to go slower and take the time to explain to the customer what work had actually been done and why. Poof! Sales growth, improved customer satisfaction and loyalty—and oh, by the way, guys liked it too.

• • •

The crossroads of the world of automotive is the car showroom. Today's tremendous pressure on price puts tremendous pressure on tactics, rather than relationships. There are only three levers to pull in the sale of a car: the price the dealer asks for it; the cost of the financing; the value of the trade-in. If you bring the price of the car down, then the dealer doesn't give you quite as good a deal on the trade-in. About the time the dealer started really investing in service and maintenance of the cars he was selling, the car companies also brought the financing in-house. So, if the dealer offers "zero percent financing," then he's not going to negotiate very much on the original price or the trade-in.

Because of the price sensitivity of the marketplace—it's pretty easy to compare by just scanning a newspaper or checking a Website—and the glut of really good cars available (both new and "previously owned"), just selling cars becomes a difficult way to make a living. So the expansion of the business to include financing, service and maintenance provides a much needed boost to the dealership. It allows the dealer to fully pull any lever he wants. Slash price with red-tag-day sales. No problem. How about zero percent financing? Okay. Or guaranteed high price for your trade-in? Terrific. He's got three ways to make the deal, like the three-card monte guys on the street corner: You're going to be snookered, but it's a fun game and at the end you get to keep the car, and talk about the deal you wrested from the salesman.

Even Ian, when he bought his new Porsche, described it to me in terms of the deal he'd negotiated for it—not the joy of the drive, or the smell of the leather or the sound of the engine when he shifts into fifth gear. Nope. How cheaply he got it, this most expensive of luxuries at whatever price. Nobody driving around suburban Atlanta needs a Porsche to crawl along the highway at rush hour. So why not just revel in the raw unnecessariness of it? The glory of its Porscheness? Why seek the rationale of "winning" out against the salesman's wiles?

Once he acknowledged that he was guilty as charged, Ian explained, there are actually any number of occasions in the car-buying process to create word of mouth, both positive and negative. The basic balance toggles between what he terms "emotional motivators" and "practical inhibitors." If the dealer makes price concessions, he can overcome the practical inhibitor and allow us to give in to our emotions. But it's not designed to create a relationship; instead, it just seems like we're haggling over price and we can do that anywhere, with any dealer. And, the word of mouth is going to be about the haggle, not the car.

In order to offset these concessions, the dealer may decide to increase the price he charges for service and repair. But that encourages us to take our cars for service elsewhere, and also reduces our relationship with the dealership. The word of mouth becomes a buzz about price-gouging practices.

So the dealer decides to bring finance and insurance in-house, which, of course, complicates the transaction and blurs our understanding of the company's image. We tell people about how the dealer handled everything, but we found out later that our bank would have done it for X percent vs. the dealer's Y percent. Still nothing about the car.

We've also seen dealers who add entirely new vehicle lines to their showrooms, reducing their credibility as experts on a certain kind of car. Or the ones who reduce sales staff and work hard to compress the amount of time on the transaction, thereby creating a precipitous decline in customer satisfaction. And, of course, there are the dealers who participate in corrupt practices, which only further erodes their and the industry's reputation.

"Here's how it works now," Ian tells me. "It's called Spot Sale, Spot Delivery." This means that you walk in the door and the salesman asks you what kind of car you're looking for. You say maybe an Explorer or an Expedition, but you're going to look at the Toyota dealership down the street, too. Maybe a Pathfinder.

You're going to go to the Lincoln-Mercury dealership, too, because a friend just got the Mercury Mountaineer. And there's that new Jeep Commander. You're calm, you're independent, above the fray. You're not really going to buy anything today. You're just looking. Right? Yeah, right.

The sales guy then says something like, "What color?" Understand, please, that he's been trained to get to the discussion of color with you in 20 seconds. Twenty seconds. You poor thing.

You say, Black with gray leather interior. Well, gosh, before you can pat your wallet pocket, he's saying, "You know, let me check." He looks a a little worried, like maybe he's just sold the last one.

Now you're worried, maybe they don't have one! He's your friend, though. He goes over to his computer and sure enough, there's a steel gray Explorer and an Anthracite Expedition, each with pewter interior, sitting on the lot right this minute. You can go for a test drive! And just before you settle in, he asks to photocopy your driver's license and for one or two other pieces of information, so he can check about financing. Well, sure, fine, after all, you're not buying anything today. It doesn't cost anything for him to check on the financing. You need to know what the payments would be. So it's no hassle when he asks for your car keys too, so he can take a good look at your current car.

While you're taking your test drive—an activity designed to "get you in the ether"—he's checking your credit, calculating the value of your trade-in and preparing a package for you. When you come back in, after listening to the gorgeous stereo surround system, imaging what you're friends will say when they see you drive it, inhaling that exotic fragrance of newness, of soon-to-be-yourness, has he got a deal for you.

Your credit has been approved, he's going to give you a good deal on your old car—you're going to arm-wrestle him a bit off the sticker price and he's going to let you. He's getting the financing at

4 percent, he's selling it to you at 8 percent. You're going to say, "Gee, I don't know, I need to check with my credit union," but all of a sudden you're not talking about "if" but "how." You're well down the road. And it's a road you can see yourself on immediately.

Spot Deal. Okay, it's not quite black, but it's cool. You could get a better deal on the financing, perhaps you should sell your own car yourself. But, gee, it would take so long. Don't forget that friend of a friend who tried to sell his car himself. The check bounced and the guy who bought couldn't be tracked down. Plus there's the indignity of driving around in a car with a For Sale sign in the window. Forget it. You're in the ether. Spot Delivery. It's on the lot. You could drive it off now. The monthly payments are within your budget, if a bit more than you've been spending. He can switch your insurance with the flick of his wrists on the keyboard.

You've just bought a car. And, as Ian points out, the day after you buy a car, you're thinking about your next car. And you're doing something else: You're reading the print advertising about this car: You bought it in a frenzy, but you can't explain that to anyone, exactly. So, you need to read up on it, so you can spout its zero-to-sixty pedigree, its horsepower, its four-wheel-drive option. But until you do that homework, you'll talk about the price and the deal.

The dealer must make a living, pay for his inventory, compensate his salespeople, hire, train and reward his mechanics. He deserves to make money on every car he sells. Ian knows this. In fact, he's the guy behind many, many successful showrooms and dealerships around the country. It's just that he's a customer too. He believes he needs to haggle on price and get a great deal, as part of the entire joy of the transaction. So Ian plays the game with the sales guy. Which walnut shell will the pea be under?

Now what's fun for Ian and a sales guy is fresh hell for me. Why? Well, I'm a woman, for starters. And everything in a car dealership screams "You're getting in over your head" to me. Women for years were the unseen presence in the showroom. No saleswomen, of course. But also there was that feeling of being absolutely invisible, the salesman seeing you, but looking through you to find the man behind you he could speak with, haggle with, play the game with.

The feeling is accurate: Women didn't matter for generations, despite our dual-income households and two-car garages, our respect for safety and valuing of—and paying for—the elements of a car designed to protect our children, our fundamental interest in the "up-charge" elements, like leather interiors, trim colors and mapping devices. We knew we were *personae non grata* in the dealerships. We could smell the burnt coffee in the waiting rooms from miles away. We knew the women's room wasn't for ladies. We knew the dog-eared magazines and tool shilling calendars in the mechanics' area would upset us if we saw them close-up.

The Internet changed all that. Women can now enter this world, seemingly alone, but armed with information from the Internet. We're not going to play the game; we're going to change the game. However, the information we're most typically armed with is price. Thus, we are being taken seriously, but we too evaluate the dealership and its cars based on the price we can demand they meet.

It puts me in mind of the way women shop for their wedding dress for almost their entire young lives, a crescendo that builds until they actually buy it, while guys focus their aspiration on that first car. Just as the wedding industry has its magazine guides, there's major media to coach guys: *Road & Track, Car and Driver, Motor Trend,* plus J. D. Powers and newspaper columns devoted to reviews of models. There are bridal fairs for women and car shows for guys. But the tough reality is that for most people, buying a car has become the moral equivalent of buying your wedding dress in Loehmann's basement. You're pretty sure you got a good deal, but you had to undress in front of everyone. And, let's face it, you're not going to take the dress back to Loehmann's to have it dry-cleaned and stored after the big day.

Price in the car showroom should just not be that important when you consider how dependent we are on the dealership for its commitment to maintain and service our cars—how "married" to them we become. If we demand cheap from them now, how will they provide the emergency service we need later? How do we imagine a dealer can pay for the talent, the service sensibility, the ethical involvement of his people, if we're unwilling to invest in it ourselves?

At Lexus, they knew that the world didn't really need another elite-car company. Toyota developed Lexus to compete with Mercedes and BMW, but the company knew that these cars are all uniformly wonderful, spectacularly engineered, thoughtfully designed. So why bother to attempt to crack this lucrative luxury world? Why invent an entirely new brand, Lexus, to appeal to people who were already thrilled by the marquee value of the competition?

Toyota reasoned that no one would pay $50,000 for a Toyota, no matter how well crafted. It created Lexus to be everything that Mercedes and BMW were, plus one more thing: thrillingly serviced. By this I mean the kind of service that makes you believe again in the dignity of a genuine work ethic, in the pride of a job well done. The kind of service that means you'll never buy another kind of car, never buy from another dealership. At whatever the price, the cost would just be too steep.

"We worked hard at this," recalls Matthew Gonzalez, from Toyota. "We knew we'd gotten it right when we started getting testimonials from owners. One story I remember particularly well was a woman whose Lexus wouldn't start one morning around 6 a.m. She was going to run to a nearby store for milk for breakfast and the car just wouldn't start. She had to get the kids to school. She had to get to work herself. So she called the dealership, just to leave a message on the machine in order to start the ordeal of getting a loaner car, getting this one in for repair.

"Instead of a machine, a real person answered the call. He told her he'd come in early, that he'd come right over and fix the car in her garage if he could. If not, he'd give her the loaner car right on the spot, so she could go about her business. If he needed to, he'd stay with the car until a tow truck could come over and bring it in for repair. Obviously, she was floored. In fact, he got there, repaired the car quickly and she was back on course for the day— and he brought a quart of milk with him. There was, of course, no charge for the repair, or the milk, for that matter."

What is that kind of service worth?

It's the kind of thing that sparks joyous word of mouth. The woman couldn't wait to tell people this story. But Lexus also created the culture in which that mechanic felt it was his duty to behave this way—and the company worked hard to celebrate such behavior, so that everyone who works there takes pride in everyone else who works there. *Shopportunity!* ratified.

Ian tells me that part of what's wrong about the industry right now is the physical design of the dealerships. There's a separation of sales and service that is indefensible, he explains. If the central core of the building allowed the customer to see the cars being worked on there'd be tremendous trust and credibility automatically. If the salesperson's job continued as your customer service representative after the sale, there'd be hope too that you're not just yesterday's sales goal, but a long-term client. If the reception area seating in the sales area also served as the waiting area for maintenance and service customers, there would be a natural give-and-take among potential and current customers that would underscore the excellence of the dealership through spontaneous word of mouth.

As it is right now, we read only of deals: of two years' free gas with a car purchase, of 50,000 mile warranties, of zero percent financing, of red-tag sales, of guaranteed new car pricing, of guaranteed trade-in allowances. All of it: a pea under the shell and you're meant to get confused. You're being taught that price is the only thing that matters, while General Motors and Ford lay off tens of thousands of our fellow workers, and renegotiate promised pensions.

Does it need to be that way? Well, let's just say that while American car companies are in a freefall, Toyota has been able to increase the actual cost we're willing to pay for its cars, provide stellar service, honor its commitments to employees, introduce new and interesting vehicles—and function as a profitable, well-managed company.

So, Rule 18, Research, search and compute the value of deep convenience beyond price. There's liberation in knowing somewhere to get dinner, fresh coffee and a smile, all the while filing up your gas tank on the way home from work. It's a freedom worth paying for, like the choice to be comfortable while you're getting that oil change on your way to your daughter's ballet class on Saturday morning. What's the sticker price on the surety that someone's going to be there for you when the tire goes flat, or the battery dies or something under the hood refuses to purr some January midnight?

Rule #18: Calculate the Value Beyond Price

And, Rule #19. Consider how that smiling salesman who welcomes you now for Spot Sale, Spot Delivery will really treat you in a year, when something has gone wrong. March right in to the mechanics' area and look at the waiting room. Imagine yourself calling the person behind the counter to beg for help some winter

morning. Ask to use the restroom for service and repair customers. It's often quite different from the one in the sales area.

Rule #19: Invest in Relationships, Not Cheap Transactions

Get the exact car you want, not the one they want to sell you to
make their numbers today. The same four-point formula that
works in the gas station convenience store should work here: people, place, principles and processes. Check them out, even as you
read the car reviews and harbor lust in your heart for that specific
model you know will make you happier, sexier, cooler. Buy it from
a dealer who is prepared to value you today, tomorrow and forever. Like a good marriage: for better *and* worse.

Now then, let's move on to the world where operators are
standing by to help us, any hour of the day or night.

Twelve

Infomercials, Home Shopping and Web Sites: When Virtual Shopping Beats Real Shopping

There came a moment in about 1988 when Bill Guthy, a theology school graduate-cum-entrepreneur, noticed something was amiss. He had started his small company, Cassette Productions Unlimited, right out of college. He was used to making copies of audio tapes for the scores of other entrepreneurs who moved across the American landscape, from hotel ballroom to hotel ballroom, touting ways to buy real estate with no money down, create mastery of your personal destiny, or achieve smooth skin with a system used by celebrities, but now made available to you, right now, for a limited time only.

A typical order from the local promoter was for 50 or 100

copies of the tape series, shipped directly to the Hilton or Embassy Suites for sale at the back of the room. The "world famous speaker and authority" took out full page ads in the local newspaper and sold admission to the lecture. There were a great many of these guys traveling the circuit in the 1980s and Bill knew most of them.

Participants didn't just read about the expert or see him interviewed on television or buy his book, they were in the same room with him. He told his personal stories, his associates worked the room through "breakout sessions" to make his message work its way into everyday lives. At the end of the seminar, attendees didn't want to let go of the connection, so they went to the back-of-the-room sales area and bought audio or video tapes. They chatted with other enthusiasts with whom they'd shared an experience. They belonged.

All of a sudden Bill started getting requests for 1,000 tapes, 2,500, even 10,000 copies at a time, and he knew something was up. Bill investigated and learned that some of these guys had taken their show to television, buying 30 minutes of time late at night, to broadcast the basic spiel and then having operators standing by to take orders for the full tape series. It was the dawn of the infomercial era.

As a fan of Napoleon Hill's *Think and Grow Rich,* Bill paid attention to this phenomenon. He enlisted a friend, Greg Renker, and they convinced Tony Robbins, of *Personal Power* fame, to take his empowerment system into this new medium. The rest, as they say, is history. Guthy-Renker is now a $1.5 billion global entity. At any moment, you stand a very good chance of being able to catch one of their hits: Victoria Principal's *Principal Secret, Proactiv Solution, Winsor Pilates, Meaningful Beauty,* and a score of others—including, improbably enough, the *Dean Martin Celebrity Roasts.*

This transformation in salesmanship was not solely a function of cheap remaindered television spot time offered in the dead of night. It was made possible by a decision on the part of the sellers to maintain an emphasis on one-on-one salesmanship—despite their emerging mass media reach. How? Through those wonderful operators, standing by at all hours of the day and night, facilitating a powerful social experience despite the fact that the shoppers were a bit groggy and in their jammies.

"We don't sell soap," Greg Renker tells me by phone from Palm Desert, California, where the company has always been based. "We sell hope. And if you sell hope, you can sell all the soap you can hope for." He tells me it's a quote from the founder of Amway, Rich DeVos, but still. The proof is in the profit: Hope is worth more than soap.

The basic four-point syntax of selling via infomercial is brutally simple: I was in worse shape than you were, I worked hard and found a way out, it's replicatable, follow me. Whether it's a product designed to get you on your way financially, or a pathway to perfect skin, each of these four bases of the sell must be tagged, in order.

"Part of the power is in the myth," says Greg. "We want the story, the narration, we want to know the creation story of the product. Customers want to know its genesis: Who created this product and why. Who uses it? We have 30 minutes to tell our story. It's a luxury many products don't have. The best product is the one that delivers the best story. Our way of looking at it is to say, 'Feel, Felt, Found.' In other words, I know how you feel, I felt that way too, until I found . . .

"Part of the power is our spokespeople. These are people who really use the product. Of course we pay for an endorsement, but not to get endorsers to use the product. For example, our Proactiv product really is used by Jessica Simpson and Puff Daddy. Once they let us know that, we start working on coming up with an endorsement deal, but we don't do it the other way around."

Each of the celebrities Guthy-Renker uses gets a *Q* ranking from an independent ranking firm: The *Q* score indicates "likability," and, according to Greg, this market rewards likability. These endorsers become that first best face of the product. It's where the human relationship between seller and buyer is formed.

He has research to prove that people watch the same infomercial over and over again, enjoying both the personality and the predictability of the show. After a point, they order. And even after they do, they keep watching. This is an amazing phenomenon, really, watching the exact same people extolling the exact same virtues of the exact same product.

"A big part of the power is the personality of the operators," he tells me. "We lose money on TV every day of the week but that's not a problem. Our customers have grown used to ordering by phone and online. We don't need to make our money every night on every show; we're looking now for products that can sustain a long-term commitment from the shopper."

Once shoppers commit to calling the 800 toll-free number on their TV set, they are really in a good place to accept an even better deal on automatic reordering. If Proactiv does clear up a lifelong struggle with acne, well, wouldn't you want it sent to you automatically every month? Of course you would. And if you order now, gosh! you get free shipping and handling.

"No great offer can overcome a bad product," says Greg, reasonably enough. "What's crucial is finding a product that works and treating it and its buyers respectfully. We encourage salespeople to spend time on the phone with the customer, to set the expectations, to enhance every step of the process. It's not a transaction, designed to be sped through on a script; it's the beginning of a long-term relationship."

It's with the free shipping and handling offer that infomercials provide the "call to action," the immediacy, indeed, the urgency to act now. Sometimes they offer a gift with purchase, as well, but in general they are not discounting the product, only the process through which you're going to acquire it the first time. Once you're on the automatic replenishment scheme, you're committed. It's no longer about shipping and handling.

The process beyond "feel, felt, found" is one of empathy at every step in the path. Unlike their retailing counterparts, infomercial marketers know that you need to stay "in the ether" in order to commit to the process. So training those 800-line operators is a major element to delivering the magical, relational interchange you crave at three in the morning.

"I'm so glad you called!" or "I'm here to help you" are greetings you'll come to expect, far afield from the dour sales clerk at the drugstore from whom you might more typically buy a skin-care product. Far more personal than a mere order taker, your guide is going to encourage you to make the commitment, maybe even offer a special deal if you act now. She thinks this is the best product. Why, she uses it herself! Pretty soon, you're handing over the credit card number and hoping that you won't have to wait four to six weeks to get your first shipment.

Greg is agnostic about how his products are ordered. Sometimes it's via an infomercial, sometimes in a mall kiosk, sometimes by having one of this stable of stars appear on a home shopping show. There are 380 Proactiv kiosks in malls around the country. There are also special selling events on Home Shopping Network and QVC.

These direct selling television channels are every bit as remarkable as the infomercial process. Under hypnosis, shoppers wax lyric about the practice. "It starts just by watching," Cheryl tells us. "You watch and watch and begin to trust the hosts. They seem more like friends. Then, there comes a point, it seems inevitable, that there's something you really need—and they only have 23 of them left. For me, it was a black pearl ring and earring set.

"My mother-in-law's birthday was coming and I knew she'd

love it, so I ordered it. I watched as the number dropped to 16 and then I just couldn't resist. The woman on the phone was so enthusiastic about it. She just couldn't have been sweeter. She agreed it would be a wonderful gift—in fact, she'd bought one when they first went on sale!—but she did tell me that I should order two, because it was so lovely, I'd want one for myself. I didn't listen. And sure enough, when it arrived, I didn't want to give it to my mother-in-law. It was just two days after I ordered it and the FedEx man came up the walk. It was so thrilling. I tried to order another one for myself, but they were all gone. It was a mistake I won't make again."

Again and again, loyal Home Shopping Network and QVC patrons talk about the entire sales progression: the hosts they love and have come to trust; the time sensitivity to certain offers; the limited quantities; the need to act now; the friendly operators standing by who are knowledgeable about the offering, encouraging and personable; even the FedEx or UPS delivery guy walking up the sidewalk is part of the thrill. And once the one item has been delivered, you really want to start the process all over again. "It's something to look forward to," Cheryl explains. "They are all so nice. It's comforting to know something is on its way to me. Everyone likes a gift and each one of these seems like a little gift, just for me."

It's really pretty spectacular how this virtual *Shopportunity!* from the depths of one's bedroom or television room becomes such a "trip" for shoppers. They speak of it as exciting and adventurous and personal, just like a great *Shopportunity!,* with tremendous anticipation and even pursuit embedded in the experience. Certainly, the process isn't about low price, although everything is characterized as an amazing deal.

Shoppers shop over and over again, some of them amassing scores of jewelry, figurines, computers, Christmas decorations and learning systems that go almost directly into the "QVC closet," as several women termed it. It's the process they love, the engagement with seemingly in-the-know and caring "consultants."

But objects aren't the only things we buy without leaving home. There's a specialty foods business, ranging from Harry & David fruit baskets to Neiman-Marcus "Mansion on Turtle Creek" meals to Philly Cheese Steaks, Peet's Coffees and Graeter's Ice Cream (legendary in Cincinnati and now available through the mail). Catalog sales, of course, are a major part of the retail economy, but I'm interested in the direct mail alternative to grocery shopping, so I call up an old friend, Todd Simon, great-great-grandson of the founder of Omaha Steaks. With grocery stores on every corner and butcher shops dotting the landscape, why order food by mail?

I met Todd when I was working on A.1. Steak Sauce several years ago. We were developing a program with Delta Airline's first class service and wanted to have great steaks served onboard, along with A.1., of course. So I flew to Omaha to meet with him and was instantly charmed. Todd is a real foodie. And he's grown up in the business.

"Our research shows that there are about 12 percent of meal occasions that we can credibly go after," he tells me. "We're looking to grow our 'share of stomach.' People have talked for generations, inviting friends over for 'Omaha steaks.' It's the dad's role: He does the steaks. About a decade ago, we started wondering about appealing more directly to women. So we created A la Zing as a meal preparation alternative: They like to eat at home, but don't want to do the entire meal from scratch. They also don't want to use more than two appliances. And they want the meal created in 25 minutes or less."

A la Zing is perfectly poised to deliver on those wants: convenience without compromise. In Todd's mind, the division doesn't compete with Omaha so much as it creates family meal occasions in preference to eating out, taking out or driving through. "With eating out, it's the expense; taking out gets the food home cold, but it's still expensive; and fast food is certainly fast and convenient, but it provides a lingering guilt that's hard to assuage."

Todd also attempted to create a very upscale division, called Five Leaf, which brought the finest restaurant—think French Laundry and Restaurant Daniel—meals to your home, but at $30 to $40 a meal per person, including appetizer and entrée, it ran head-on into the price barrier. At those rates, patrons wanted the "theater," as he describes it, of the restaurant setting. But he learned valuable lessons.

"We don't have consumer service reps," he tells me. "We have meal consultants. These are professionals who know food and enjoy our wares. They speak with knowledge and authority as well as enthusiasm with our customers. We work hard to ensure that the ordering experience, whether on the phone or online, is enjoyable and educational. We take it seriously and our customers respond to that."

The response is so strong—A la Zing has doubled its sales every year—that Todd is now moving into retail in malls, creating a "meal center" for shoppers who want to kick their food shopping up a notch. Note to grocery stores: He's not promoting on price, but on taste, convenience and educating the palate. Why isn't this customer turning to you for this wisdom?

This shopper engages in a virtual *Shopportunity!* in preference to one in an actual grocery store precisely because of the engagement, knowledge and enthusiasm of the sales consultants. And why would an A la Zing or Harry & David customer be willing to move from catalog and online sales into a mall, rather than a grocery store? For exactly the same reason. People, people, people. A social connection that imparts knowledge and enthusiasm: priceless.

•   •   •

This move of catalog and online sales into physical retail space seems counterintuitive to my mind. But Missy Park is doing it with Title 9, and Todd Simon is doing it here. Doug Raboy, Adam Hanft's colleague at Hanft-Raboy Partners advertising firm, knows about as much as anyone I've met about the seamless integration of online and offline presence. He's the visionary behind the AT&T Wireless Website, Hertz.com, Virgin Mobile.com, and Match.com.

"The Internet is a very good place to lie," he tells me, quoting Clotaire Rapaille, with whom the company worked to 'crack the code' on AT&T Wireless. "The trick is to gain people's trust and that means spending time with them, making the sites extremely organic and reducing the reasons they have to just quit the experience. The way we do that is by creating a reference point. With AT&T it was easy. We just called it the 'biggest store.' Shoppers had an understanding of what they liked and didn't like about shopping for a cell phone. We worked to give them more about what they liked—the techno-lust of getting the newest, latest—and reducing the high pressure, 'I've got to make my sales goal' tactics."

Hanft-Raboy unearthed the "thing behind the thing" in cell phone sales: There's still such magic in the phone, it makes the cell phone owner feel like a superhero. With it, he or she can do anything. The goal for the company was simply to get them to the magic in the most comfortable way possible, including sending two phones to the undecided shopper, with a self-mailer to return the unwanted one.

"Everyone knows that when you buy a cell phone in a conventional store, the salesman goes into the back room and does something to the phone to activate it," Doug tells me. "We found out that 'magic' was a stumbling block to online ordering, because there was the fear that when the phone arrived, you'd still have to take it to the shop and have the guy do something to it in the back room. So, we used flash design technology in the Web site enabling shoppers to literally 'play' with the phone and we promise that it will arrive ready to use."

"The Web is the big highway," Doug Shouse, president of Coyne Beahm Shouse, tells me. "Those of us doing Web marketing have moved beyond driver's ed and into our first real car. We're exhilarated, but a bit tentative. Done right, Web marketing allows us to *engage* with the brand and one another authentically and intensely. The sites that get it? Check out converse gallery.com; miniusa.com; and smokerswelcome.com. It's not about passivity or interruption. It's about building brand democracies."

The tone these sites use to communicate with their visitors is gripping, really. Straightforward, clear, creative, cogent, respectful. And Shouse's word "engaged." You're not sitting idly here. You want to participate, to make your own Converse film (or at least to forward one to friends, or at least to buy the shoes), to design your own Mini Cooper, to complain vehemently with other smokers about the restrictions you face. These sites want you and need you to be there. If there's something you don't like, they want to know. You become a part of this world, which Shouse tells me isn't a virtual reality anymore, it's its own reality. The Web is creating brand democracies in which we all vote.

Having purchased a Dell printer via the Internet to endless frustration and ultimate fury, I am intrigued by the idea of consumer service that encourages and facilitates contact. It is, of course, important to point out that solid customer service in any medium is a rarity. One 2005 study reports that only 33 percent of people who deal with consumer service representatives are satisfied—and that 18 percent say they resort to yelling at the person on the other end of the phone.

My own experience attests to this. I wanted a laser printer that could print out this manuscript quickly for me, as I was writing. Dell seemed to offer a very good model at a fair price. I ordered it and tracked it on the Web site to see when it would arrive. So far, so good. It arrived with an instruction manual, but no disc for syncing my Sony Vaio to the printer. I went on the Web site and looked up that exact problem. The site told me that a trained expert was not available to help me, so I should call the 800 line. Okay. Here's what happened next.

"Your call is important to us. Please hold on."

Well, of course. Twelve minutes later, with this message repeated roughly every 15 seconds, interspersed with mind-numbing music, a consumer services rep came on the line, seemingly from somewhere in New Delhi.

"Thank you for calling Dell. How may I assist you."

"I just received my Dell printer, but there is no computer disc to sync it to my computer."

"Are you sure?"

"Yes."

"You've checked the packaging material?"

"Yes."

"Please hold on."

We're back to the "your call is important to us" Muzak recording, for another eight minutes.

"Thank you for holding. Your call is important to us. I want to make sure we give you the very best consumer service. Your call may be recorded. Can you tell me your serial number?"

I tell him the number.

"Let me repeat that." He does, correctly.

"Would you mind holding for another few moments?"

We're back to the recording. Four minutes later, he reappears.

"Thank you for holding. Your call is important to us. Let me repeat your serial number." He does.

"Yes, that's right."

"And you're sure that the disc is not in the packing materials."

"Yes."

"That's very strange. Is there anything else I can help you with?"

"What?"

"I'm unable to assist you at the moment. I'm very sorry. But my computer is not able to access the information. You'll need to call back later. Is there anything else I can help you with?"

"No. That's the problem. No disc. Can't you just send me one?"

"Are you sure it wasn't in the packing materials?"

"Yes! I'm sure."

"You checked?"

"Yes!"

"I'm sorry. I can't help you further with this issue right now. I am committed to giving you the highest quality consumer service. Tell me, how would you rank Dell's service at this time, on a scale of one to 10 with 10 being outstanding and one being substandard."

"I don't think you want to ask me that right now."

"I'm sorry. I don't understand. It would help me if I could gauge your opinion of our consumer service. Dell is committed to providing outstanding customer service."

"What should I do?"

"About what?"

"About getting the disc for the printer, to sync to my computer."

"I'm sorry. I'm very sorry. But I can't access that request for you now."

"So, I'm supposed to call back later?"

"You could do that, but I'm wondering if you could just take a few minutes to take a brief questionnaire."

"I'm going to hang up now."

This is pretty nearly verbatim. I couldn't possibly make it up. I called back several times over the next several weeks, sometimes getting a man, sometimes a woman, all equally unable to help me because of computer problems on their end in accessing the information. At one point, I had yelled so angrily at a woman that she began calling me back to monitor the situation. Unfortunately, she was ill-informed about the time difference between my home office and India and I was awakened at three in the morning by her concerned follow-up. The disc was reportedly sent three or four times, and arrived once.

Equally astounding was the situation with Sprint, when I ordered a pair of walkie-talkies for my mother, while she was recovering from that very serious illness, and my brother. It was imperative that they stay in contact, if he had to leave her bedside, and I hoped that walkie-talkies would do the trick. I ordered them and sent them down. My brother, however, was not up to the task of setting them up, so they were never used.

Suddenly, I started getting bills of about $163 per phone, per month. Naturally, I called Sprint to recount the problem, relatively sure I'd get an apology and a prompt deduction from my AmEx card.

"Thank you for calling Sprint, now with Nextel. Please hold. Your call is important to us." Well, you get it, more Muzak. At the end of the conversation, I was enraged. They'd automatically activated my account and charged the balance due to American Express, and planned to do that for the next 18 months. Even though the phones had never been unpacked from the box. So, I called American Express, which blessedly agreed to deal with them for me. American Express did, indeed, get that charge removed, but the next month, there it was again. So, I packed up the phones and found the snail mail address of the president and sent them to him. After six months of silence, my account was finally credited.

It's the heavily scripted consumer service protocol that makes us cringe when we have to deal with a human being and heave a sigh of relief when we can handle an issue via technology. Lynne Crump-Caine, who runs her own business, Outside In Consulting, says that an empowered workforce capable of making on-the-spot resolutions to consumer problems is the ultimate business asset in today's retail economy. It's also a rarity.

Both Greg Renker and Todd Simon are passionate about what they do, and they hire equally passionate people, treating them like real people capable of dealing well with customers, and occasionally of making mistakes. Humanity is a messy business and when we attempt to take the humanity out of the shopping experience, via scripts and computer screens that anticipate and overrule human judgment, we create computerized responses that disappoint and infuriate.

When we bother to train, pay and reward real people, we get honest advocates whose authenticity and care comes right through the phone line, and making us, the shopper, want to reward them too, with our order. Over and over again, as I've interviewed people for this book, it's that human interaction that prompts the sale and loyalty to the store: The most frequent quote: "She'd been so kind to me, I had to buy it." The shopper knows her part of the relationship: The store, whether virtual or physical, needs to deliver on its part.

Certainly, some Internet sites require no human interference. Think eBay and Amazon. Even my beloved FreshDirect. They simply avoid the whole chaotic need for a relationship between people, preferring to correspond through automated gestures, which is grand. These sites don't promise a human-to-human interaction; rather they provide a deeply customized, automated and friendly process as designed by computer programmers. The process is constantly improved and expanded, remaining profoundly intuitive and pleasant. That's all they promise and it's precisely what they deliver.

When we enter this virtual world, we learn quickly and then expect to release any expectation of productive and empathetic human interaction. We rely instead on the profound utility, speed and adventure of an empathetically designed site. Drugstore.com is one such I've come to love. It automatically remembers my orders, encourages me to spend $6 more on additional products so that I can qualify for free shipping, and reminds me when I'm probably out of shampoo. It also sends me emails to tell me that I've "earned" money to be used on my next order, prompting me to return before I would remember to go.

The physical bricks-and-mortar world of retailing doesn't promise the speed, efficiency, and unflappable niceness of a computer program. Rather, it provides the traditional "catch-as-catch-can" of sometimes exhilarating, sometimes goofy sales help to coach us through or ignore us. The best shopping provides that elusive experience of getting great wares in a great environment from great experts and, at the end of the day, feeling better about ourselves for having done so. It's troubling that some days a computer is more humane than a human.

The real problem is when the two shopping universes collide: when we expect the sanity of a rationally developed software program to anticipate our wants and needs and respond to us personally and we get instead a human automaton trying his or her damnedest to follow a script, regardless of our situation. Infomercials, home-shopping and direct-mail marketers may have once been the stepchildren of business, but there's no denying that they are outperforming the blue-chip firms at this crucial and fragile moment of delivering the dream.

So, Rule #20. Reward the personal. Any firm that can't or won't provide you with real help (human or automated) to coach you through the process does not deserve your business. There are a great many wonderful products in our world—laser printers, cell phones, skin care—you don't need to buy the ones that don't value their wares enough to stand behind them, or value you enough to work to earn your enthusiasm when things go wrong.

Rule #20: *Reward the Personal*

And Rule #21: Make the seller pay for dissing you. Seller be-ware—we're fed up and we're not going to take it anymore. Any company that won't put you first needs to be complained to and about. Scream it to the world. Tell your friends. Report it to the Better Business Bureau. Email me and I'll post it on my Website. Do *something*.

Rule #21: *Make the Seller Pay for Dissing You*

It's just not acceptable to suck the meaning out of the poten-tial partnership the shopper and seller have the power to create to-gether. If we're doing our part as shoppers, then there's an obligation on the seller's part to step up to the plate. When they don't, it becomes our job again to call them on it. To force ac-countability. We're part of a consumer society, after all. We need to be good citizens.

Section Three: Summary

21 Steps to Become a
Retail Revolutionary

Perhaps you are shopping right now. Perhaps you have turned to this chapter to help you make the decision whether or not to purchase this book. There are "blurbs" from well-known experts on the cover. There is a huge $23.95, which is undoubtedly not the price you'll pay for the book. Perhaps you're dissatisfied with your shopping experiences. You've reached out to this title, searching for a genuine *Shopportunity!* But, you're undecided. My advice: Use these 21 rules to determine whether this is the book for you.

1. Relearn Anticipation

Is this a book you've looked forward to reading? A topic you're engaged by? Let's look forward to each thing we're going to acquire. It may seem impossible when confronted with aisles of books, toothpaste, moisturizers and dish soaps, but we need to reconnect to the essential magic of these products. Imagine, for a moment, life without them. Create this habit in the small choices and it will be there to help you enjoy the big purchases, like a child at Christmas. It's there for us, if we'll just claim it.

2. Enjoy Your Choices

In every bookstore you have hundreds of thousands of books from which to choose: Self-help, Psychology, Religion, Fiction, Business, Pop Culture. Relax and luxuriate in such abundance. There is learning all around you.

In every grocery store, you have 50,000 choices to make; in every Big Box store, 100,000. Visualize that. Most of us shut down and move through the aisles on autopilot, avoiding those we can, minimizing those we must make into a standard rote path: See it, know it, buy it. But why eradicate our time in stores? Why ignore the cultural transformations happening around us? We don't have to make our own soap. Hell, we don't even have to be home to answer our phone. We can have any one of virtually a million different cars, an act of unprecedented creation that makes it uniquely ours, through its color, upholstery, striping, audio system and gear-box ornamentation. Investigate, educate, explore, enjoy: Celebrate.

3. Let Brands Transform You

Certainly, this book seeks to help you transform from a harried buyer to an engaged investigator. Books and brands are willing to do it; they will take you from overachieving, high-powered executive to besotted parent, just when you need them to. They'll help you make the move from underage adolescent to fine-wine connoisseur if you give them the time and attention they deserve.

They'll even help you tell the world that you're out of the child-tending business and into your second adolescence if you let them. Just in that moment when you're moving from one self to the next, here comes the cavalry charge of brands to the rescue: Let them do their work.

4. Name, Frame, Claim the Transformation You Desire

There are at least three types of transformations you can expect from your brand decisions. It may be participation in a cultural transformation, an assist through a life-stage passage or the simply mood altering jolt of your caffeine of choice, but know what you're asking of a brand and what you're really getting.

This book, for example, wants so much to transform our cheapening culture into a celebration and to transform your chore list into an exploration, our mindless routines into evocative adventures.

5. Badge Intentionally

Products and brands are chockablock with meaning. They work wonderfully as language in a consumer society to tell the story of you, quickly, succinctly and well. Crucial to understand: They do it whether we ask them to or not, so best to acknowledge this badging benefit. Your watch, your shoes, your bag, your beverage, even the whiteness of your teeth telegraph your message. Make sure you're saying what you mean.

What will reading this book say about you on the bus tonight?

6. Dress for Shopping Success

It does us no service to be sloppy shoppers. The salespeople we want to help us have to dress for their jobs; when we're shopping, shopping is our job. We need to dress fittingly. There's a confidence and respect that comes from it and it's a two-way confidence: The sales person believes we're engaged in finding the right thing and that we have the taste to know it when we see it—and we know we can bear to look in the dressing-room mirror. Dressing well silences that voice within that whispers it doesn't matter or that the dress will look better when we have our hair done.

7. Buy What You Love—or Know Why Not

We're buying for others so often that we can forget to remember to evaluate our purchases ourselves: He loves this; she'll like this; they need this. That's one of the wonderful gifting aspects of things. However, a gift is often treasured because the giver loves it, has taken the time to find and share the giver's passion with the recipient. It's true in big and little purchases. So, search for a cereal you love and share it with your finicky eater. Evaluate your recipes on your taste, too. If you learn to love this book, pass it along.

8. Kick Your Addiction to Price

Cut yourself off: No more discussions of price. No more, "I got a gallon of pickles for $2.89." No more, "I got a great deal on the car." Just don't reinforce this behavior, now that you know it's sending dopamine coursing through your neurotransmitters. It's an artificial high with tremendous consequences for you and everyone else in the culture. Do you really want that jar of pickles enough to shop at a place that won't give health care or a living wage to its workers? Do you want to be buying food you never use before it molds—or equally dismal, food you feel you have to consume because it's there? Do you want to buy a car so cheaply that the dealer can't afford to stand behind it, or needs to price-gouge you on the service in order to make ends meet? No more discussions of price. Just quit, cold turkey. Reprogram yourself to discuss the details of the new purchase, the nuances, the recipes and family memories you'll make.

9. Don't Compromise on the Everyday

Buy the best in class of every single thing you buy. This doesn't necessarily mean the most expensive: It means the best. Take the time to assess each thing. It's more than letting go of the store brand cream cheese and trading up to a national brand. It's searching out the fresh chive-enhanced version in the deli counter. It's paying attention, profound consciousness. If it's worth a portion of your paycheck and time out of your life, then why not buy lotion-infused Puffs instead of no-name tissues? Buy better and you'll buy less is my guess, and you'll enjoy each purchase more.

10. Look Clerks in the Eye and Ask about Their Day

And waitresses and waiters too. And, of course, booksellers. These are people. They are not mere commodities there to be mindlessly ignored. If we want our salespeople to take an interest in us, it's only fair that we acknowledge their existence and imagine their working lives. These jobs are pretty much underpaid and thankless. We can do something about both of those things. Shop where the people are paid decently—make it your business to know if they are—and say thank you.

11. Shop Where the Staff Knows More than You

If they can't or won't help you because they simply don't know anything about what they're selling, move on. Don't reward this behavior with your business. Every single product category has experts—buying the precise book that responds to your needs, fitting a sports bra, finding the right fishing lure, searching out a Guy Lombardo recording of *Auld Lang Syne.* Go where you can learn. They're called sales help for a reason. No help. No sales.

12. Shop above Your Budget

Whatever your budget, shop above it. You don't have to buy, but you can learn mightily. Go into the best stores you can find and talk with the salespeople. Study the nuances of every potential purchase. If you're looking for new fall clothes, then go to the designer floors of your very best local department or specialty store: Bergdorf Goodman, Barneys, Neiman-Marcus, Nordstrom, Gucci, Prada, Ralph Lauren, wherever. Ask questions, understand what to look for in the style, function and wit of great design. You'll know it when you see it again in your more usual haunts. Or if you're shopping for a car, go to a Mercedes, Lexus or BMW showroom.

Two great things will happen: You'll learn a great deal about this year's styles and what appeals to you about them and you may actually find something there you can afford, perhaps one perfect something that will reinvigorate your wardrobe or a great deal on a previously-owned car that is better for you than a new, but lesser model.

13. Follow the Passion

Stores hold the personal passions of retailers within their walls. It's palpable. If the passion is for making this quarter's numbers, then you'll see it in the desperation of the continuous sales signs. If the passion is for the product, you'll feel that too. Shop where the retailer's passion meets your own. If they care about the food you're buying for your family like you do, then support them in that. If they want you to be excited by their wares because they are, encourage them with your business. One glance around most stores will tell you where their passion is. Follow it to rekindle your own.

14. Feed Your Mind

Every product has a back story. Who made it, how it is made, how it should be used. These aren't simple, interchangeable commodities, but life-enhancing essentials: extra virgin olive oil, artisanal cheeses, double-ply paper towels, tartar-control toothpaste, pull-up diapers, Each one has a reason for being and typically it is to make our lives easier and better. Each one will reward a bit of study on our part. Why not learn the pedigree of the olives you're going to put out for snacks? They traveled a long and circuitous route to arrive in your refrigerator: Let them tell the tale.

15. Seek the Ethic

Each of the stores we shop today—whether individual shop or mega chain—has some sort of ethic. Some are made clear: Whole Foods, Starbucks, Ralph Lauren, Wal*Mart, Target each hold up an ethic, a point of view they've decided to stand for. You have ethics too. What do you value? The cheapness at any cost of a Wal*Mart? The design sensibility of Target or Ralph Lauren? The Whole Foods's mission of mainstreaming organic? The vision of Starbucks's Howard Shultz to provide even part-time workers health-care and profit-sharing benefits? Go behind the scrim and figure out what these firms stand for and shop the ones with which you agree.

16. Shop Old Worlds That Are New to You

We all have a comfort zone, but really exciting things happen when we move outside them. Find a place that sells fresh pasta, or Greek cheese, or Chinese dumplings. Search out authentic chopsticks or a tiny knitting store. Get off the hamster wheel of shopping repetition and go into an area of town that's new to you. It may be purveying authentic ingredients for Mexican food or vintage blouses or esoteric crafts, but explore and expand your known world. Oh! What stories you'll have. Helen Fisher says that one of the great ways to generate dopamine is newness, novelty, fresh exciting experiences. Go for it.

17. Break Out of the Big Box

Just stop. Don't go into any Big Box store of any kind for the next 21 days. That's what Tony Robbins told me it takes to kick a habit: 21 days of doing something else. What happens? How do you cope? Where do you go? Why don't you buy? What is really essential? Make conversation with the shopkeepers at the substitute stores you find. Take your time. Did you really spend more money? Less? Did you get better advice, make a new friend? Email me and let me know.

18. Calculate Value Beyond Price

Who is going to be there for you when you need them—and what is that worth? Walgreens's advertising right now seems to sit on this promise: They'll be there for you in the middle of the night. They're not promising cheap; they're promising to help you out at your moment of need, whether it's for film, gift wrap or a prescription for a colicky baby. The On-Star roadside assistance system from General Motors promises the same kind of "we're here for you" service. Walgreens promise is a tremendous boon to the time-starved among us. On-Star lends a hand when we're at our most vulnerable, broken down on the side of the road. It is costly for these firms to be there for us 24/7, but it's undeniably precious in the moment.

19. *Invest in Relationships, Not Cheap Transactions*

There's a joy in being known. And in knowing that the dealer who sold you the car or the computer store associate who advised your most recent technology purchase will actually be there for you when you need help. Take a look around the floor and ask the salesperson how long they've been there, what kind of training they have in your particular product. Ask what happens if something goes wrong. In a car dealership, it's relatively easy to check out the service area. It's a bit harder in a consumer electronics or hardware store, but ask. Is the staff at all helpful? Is there any kind of policy to make sure you're happy with the purchase? What happens if you get it home and can't hook it up? Is there a store number to call to be coached through the process, or do they refer you to the manufacturer's Web site or 800 number. Probe the salesperson about their follow-up to the sale—and if you don't like what you hear, move on.

20. *Reward the Personal*

When you find a salesperson who "gets you," who is willing to shop the store with you, suggesting ways to enhance an outfit or a dinner party or your new outdoor furniture, stick with that person. Go back to them. Tell your friends about them. Create a personal relationship with them, so they are free to call you and tell you about a blouse they think you'd like, that they've trolled the known world and found one more table setting in your pattern at their store in Sheboygan, that they've found the chaise longue to go with the teak table and chairs, just in time for your July Fourth picnic. Wherever you find them, celebrate the people who view selling as a profession—one meant to help you make the home, business, party of your dreams.

21. Make the Seller Pay for Dissing You

It's just unacceptable when you're put on permanent hold, told to wait for 20 minutes while being assured that "your call is important to us" and then informed that you can't be helped now, because "our computers are down." Sorry doesn't cover it. The good news is that the power of word of mouth is on your side. Make sure to follow up every time that you receive unsatisfactory service. Tell the store manager, write the company president, tell six friends *and* write to me at myshopportunity.com. We're creating a database of "shops to shop" and "shops to drop." Let me know the good, the bad and the indifferent.

If you're not getting the transformational promise of brands in the stores you shop, shop elsewhere. Do the due diligence and do not reward and perpetuate shoddy, sloppy service with your patronage. The race to the bottom can be stopped, but only by us. Retailers will respond, but very few will lead—so we need to.

Epilogue

I began the writing of this book convinced that products and brands provide tremendous transformational opportunities for consumers, that the promise of these transformations is never more powerful than when we are on the cusp of acquiring the product and that it is just at that moment, when we are excited and invigorated by the product's potential, that retailers seek to convince us that price is the only thing that matters. That cheap is better.

I remain convinced of this. What has changed for me is what I think can be done about it. When I began, I thought a wake-up call for retailers was in order. But, after coming to terms with the essential paradigm shift in our psyches that has made us willing co-conspirators in this race to the bottom, I believe real change will only come when we change. When shoppers vote with their pocketbooks and refuse to be treated poorly or to buy shoddy merchandise, just because it's okay, available and cheap.

Most retailers are reactive. So long as we tell them that cheap is what we're after, cheap is what we'll get. What we want are retailers who are leaders, who trust us to respond to values beyond cheap. Clearly, Starbucks is one such. Had Howard Schultz asked people if they wanted to spend $3.50 for a cup of coffee, he'd never have opened his first shop. He gave us a home away from home and we've come home to it in droves—around the world—and all the while he's worked to pay decent salaries and benefits to his baristas, while he professionalizes the craft. Whole Foods is another company willing to lead, willing to respect its customer, willing to spend the time and money to educate them and us. Williams-Sonoma is another. So too is Ralph Lauren, which I oddly pair with Target because of their seemingly shared belief we'll respond to excellent design—and we do.

Bloomingdale's used to be a leader in department store retailing: Giants like Carl Levine, the home furnishings visionary, and Kalman Ruttenstein, the legendary fashion director, brought to bear an eclectic energizing vision, enabled by Marvin Traub, the chief executive officer whose goal was to make Bloomies truly "Like No Other Store in the World." We must mourn the loss of such a mission among the sea of sameness we wander each time we enter a mall.

I do put much of the blame for this sad state of affairs at the door of Wal*Mart and its insistence that "everyday low prices" is what we're about. But we the shoppers have to own up to our role in enabling its growth from Arkansas wannabe retailer into one of the two largest American companies in the world. We've grown it—and it has grown us, with its emphasis on cheap food and large industrial sizes.

As Joseph Nocera put it, "If we want to change Wal*Mart, we have to change ourselves first." And I have come, in the process of writing this book, to emphatically agree. We have become addicted to savings and in order to get the high we crave by saving, we must spend. In this construct, the market migrates to the bottom. Wal*Mart's price becomes the North Star by which all retailers must navigate.

In order for retailers to compete with Wal*Mart, they must shave costs out of the equation at every step along the path, including wages, training and service. These values are in a death spiral; soon there will be nothing left to cut. It will be survival of the cheapest. Few choices; low quality; no support at one end of the financial spectrum; profound and profoundly expensive goods and service at the other end. A void where the vibrant middle used to be.

It's starting already, of course. Early in 2006, Kraft announced another round of downsizing and factory closings, reportedly because people prefer to eat out. But I don't think it's just that. I think it's that we're learning to hate to shop in grocery stores, which are increasingly dirty, begrudging spaces staffed with shutdown people. Who wouldn't rather go to an Appleby's or an Olive Garden or even a Subway or just call Domino's?

We see it in the airline industry, where executives start by trying to carve out the travel agent's commission, then to forgo meals and snacks on the flights, and end up shaving wages and pensions of the very people who make it all work. We see it in our inability to have a passenger rail service that functions well enough to attract riders. We see it in the radical wave of plant closings in the American automobile industry.

Is it possible to cost-cut our way to growth? Is it possible to succeed—via a death of a thousand cuts? My favorite response to this comes from the airline industry. "If you are being rewarded for finding ways to make pizza cheaper, eventually you'll take the cheese off," says Gordon Bethune, former CEO of Continental. "You'll make it so cheap that people won't eat it."

We are coming close to that in modern American retailing.

The definition of the word "repent" as it is used in the Bible means to turn around and walk the other way. And that is what we as a culture need to do and what we as individuals must do. Every step we take farther in this direction takes us farther and farther away from the fascinating delights of the marketplace. So here's my heretical Rx: Pay people more. Give them both wages and benefits. Pay people enough that they don't have to work two jobs to make ends meet. Pay a living wage.

If I were president, this would be my "Mr. Gorbachev, tear down this wall!" moment. Captains of industry: Make better things, charge more for each thing and *pay your people a living wage.* Don't wait for the government to tell you what your minimum wage ought to be. Lead.

Pay your people a living wage. What will happen? First, every corporation will take a hit and their shareholders too, for a bit. For a couple of quarters, at least, but maybe even a year. Maybe even two. But hey! Doing business the way we've been doing it has kept the Dow hovering around 11,000 for years, sent millions of jobs offshore, eroded family life, pushed many into personal bankruptcy *and* obesity.

Pay your people a living wage. What will happen? What do people do when they have money? They spend it, they save it, they pay taxes on it. All terrific options for a consumer society. More people with more money to spend on more and better stuff. More people saving to pay for houses, cars, educations, retirements. More people paying the taxes it takes to deliver on the promises a government makes to its citizens. Not really a very sinister scenario.

Shoppers: Buy less, buy better, shop where a living wage is paid. Get out of the habit of mindlessly buying in the moment. Visualize each product latitudinally. Where did it come from, who made it, how much were they paid, what kind of conditions do they work and live in, how knowledgeable are the staff people here, are they well paid, are the bathrooms clean, how long will you use this, what will happen to it once you're done—eBay, hand-me-down, storage locker, cherished memento or one more piece of indestructible garbage nestled in the landfill? These are all questions we need to know the answers to before we acquire one more thing.

My sincere hope is that the 21 rules threaded throughout this book become your personal manifesto for revolutionizing your retail experience. We can return thrill to the hunt—and pause long enough in the process to actually enjoy the transformational promises of the products we buy. I wish you good hunting, great hunting, thrilling hunting. But not bargain hunting.

Acknowledgments

This book simply would not exist were it not for the time, talent and energies of three wonderful people. Sharlene Martin, my agent, who saw its potential in a two-page query letter and never doubted. Herb Schaffner, my editor, who understood its audience better than I did and held firm to that initial vision with thoughtful and thought-provoking questions, comments and conversation. The poet and writer Julie Sheehan, who worked with me to find the conceptual "through line" phase of the argument. To each of these three I am cheerfully indebted and grateful.

There are also a number of colleagues, friends and the occasional stranger who shared hard-won wisdom with me: Peter Connolly, Ian Rattray and Tom Magness volunteered days of their valuable time to help me see and understand what I was seeing in stores of all stripe. Charlene Margaritis, Bonnie Predd, and Laura Schenone painstakingly and lovingly deconstructed their own shopping rituals for me. Brett Stover was always at the ready to discuss his perspectives on various questions, even as he traveled the globe advising retailers from Shanghai to San Diego. We were rarely in the same time zone, but always on the same wavelength. Diane Podrasky took me behind the scenes of a fashion brand's real challenges in dealing day-to-day in the war to preserve product integrity in the face of ever-narrower margins.

On the marketing side, Faith Popcorn was, as always, the soul of generosity in sharing her vision and expertise. Having worked with her for seven years at an earlier point in my career, I never fail to be impressed with the audacity of her thinking and the static-free channel into the culture to which she is so clearly attuned. Nobody does it better. So too I must thank Adam Hanft and Doug Raboy, partners in figuring out the virtual world of retailing, as well as serious unravelers of all retailing conundrums.

Daryl Brewster, formerly of Kraft, and now running Krispy Kreme, was a voice of calm authority and clarity as I tried to figure out the various channels of trade our foods flow through. He is, without doubt, the smartest, cleanest strategic thinker and savvy realist I've met in the world of packaged goods. Kathy Parker, his VP of new products at Kraft, Margo Lowry, formerly strategy head of Kraft, and Glen Fleischer, strategic impresario: all articulate arbiters of the art of the possible in present-day grocery, club and convenience stores, as well as the power that branding brings to these marketspaces. There were several anonymous sources as well, who deconstructed today's retailing reality for me, a reality that unhappily includes mega-retailer retaliation as a risk.

Helen Fisher was graciousness itself in helping me understand the neurological components to our addiction to the cheap. Hal Goldberg and the shoppers he hypnotized (and whose names and details I changed in order to protect their privacy) unearthed with me the underpinnings, the "thing behind the thing," we search for in all shopping, from the boring routine to the resonate cultural ritual.

Missy Park, Mike Jacobsen, the brilliant Cie Nicolson, Greg Renker, Charles Fishman's articles for *Fast Company,* Gail Sheehy's *Passages,* Norris Bernstein, Rick Levine, Chris Kurjanowicz, Bob Taraschi, Terry Preskar, Peter Klein, Steve Rosenberg and Julia Christensen: All great sources of information and insight to figure a pathway out of the cheapening of the American dream, as I came to understand it. Creed O'Hanlon is one of the great minds I've met in my travels: a sterling essayist, savvy marketer and wonderful friend, despite his decision to remain ensconced in Australia. The Reverend Tim Keller, through his wife, Kathy, was always there to help me assess the spiritual implications of our quest for stuff. Doug Shouse, president of Coyne Beahm Shouse, was a terrific guide into the world of postmodern marketing. Barbara Rothberg, Ph.D., was able to impart wisdom born from her relationship-therapy practice and transfer it effortlessly into the world of brand relationships. Eve Eliot's understanding of the neurotic underpinnings of eating disorder behavior was similarly essential. Two automobile strategists, Matthew Gonzalez and Nihar Patel, could not have been more helpful, nor more clear-eyed in their discussion of the car market we confront today. Dr. Clotaire Rapaille, whose anecdotes from the annals of marketing meaning are becoming the stuff of legend, as is his charm, was able to share his look under the hood of how our reptilian brains work the strands that are woven into the fabric of brands. Lynn Crump-Caine was at her insightful best describing both her professional and personal shopping analysis. And, of course, to Ask, Google and Google Scholar: Research has never been more exciting. Thank you.

There have been also been scores of professionals who have informed my thinking by their wisdom, experience and grace: Bill

McGuire, Saul Bennett, Dick Weiner, Bob Wiener, Ed Stanton, Pauline Grieger, Pat Hayes, Carol Boyd, Jim Postl, Liz Harvey, Nancy Chandler Koglmeier, Karen Francis, Susan Knobler, François Baird, Mark Chataway, Serita Nayyar, Andy Schindler, Lynn Beasley, Fran Creighton, Scott Rhodes, Brice O'Brien, Melanie Barbee, Ronda Plummer, Mike Schott, Mark Morrissey, Richard Wyse, Jane Hunter, Eytan Urbas, Hillary Bidwell MacKay, Mechele and Sander Flaum, Claire Babrowski, Everett Fortner, Rick Lenny, Jim Kilts, Karen Barry Schwarz, Doug and Elaine Lunne, Stacey Ruben Dempsey, Erin Foster, Doug Conant, John Greeniaus, Harry Hoffman, Dara Tyson, Buzz Richmond, Mike Frazier, Seth Familian, Peggy Belanger, Judi Roaman, Mike Sinyard, Eric and Robin Eidsmo, Bentley Renker, Jim Bechtold, Charlotte Otto, John Cowles, Joe Duffy, Barbara Hulit, Lori Daniel, Phil Ziesemer, Len Taconi, Terry Campion, Tiffany Vasilchik, Jennifer Levine, Lynda Pollio, Tony Robbins, Jessye Norman, Gloria Steinem, Marie Wilson, John Hayes, Christine Brandt-Jones, Billie Brouse, Mary Kay Moment, Kathleen Cantwell, Robin McIver, David Lenefsky, Gay Haynes, Maureen Hood, Janet Siroto, Julie Larkin, Sandra Erazo, and Dr. Richard Zimmer. All come effortlessly to mind.

Naturally in any enterprise such as this, the ongoing encouragement of family and friends cannot be overstated nor overlooked. John Olsen and Doug Ray, my great friends, neighbors and Mattie's favorite playmates, could always be counted on for a fascinating conversation on any topic that tweaked my interest at the moment. Both savvy marketers, they have each confronted the difficulty of getting a brand's promise to market. Likewise, Roger Hockett and Patrick Boylan, parents of Mattie's Sunday school buddies, Nora and Luke, would talk about it endlessly with me, or change the subject, depending upon how the writing was going at the moment. Jayne Sherman and Deby Zum were equally able to bring up or avoid the topic, due in large part to the sensitivity of their friendship. John Margaritis, a steadfast voice of encouragement, was willing to share the ultimate expertise on the topic at hand, via his wife, Charlene, with whom I shopped.

Gary Kaplan, Elizabeth Hutchison, Cheryl Hironaka, Laura Fazekas, Carolina Nitsch and her husband, Deiter von Graffenried were more than passingly interested in shopping, ready to share stories and offer cogent thoughts. John Casey and Nancy Smith, parents of Roma, Bea and Frances, were early and ongoing supporters of this project and, indeed, it was through John's suggestion to visit MediaBistro.com that I stumbled upon my agent. Also, thanks too to my deep friends for many, many years: Dianne Sauder Jacobsen, Judy Baker VanderWeg, Ann Kandrac Evory, Susan London, Renee Russak, Dilys Evans, Sheila Paterson, Susan Atkins, Bobby Klimecki and Traci Godfrey.

Just about the time I signed the contract for this book, my mother, Dorothy, became gravely ill. So it is with pure happiness that I approach its publication knowing that she'll be here to read it, thanks of course to modern medicine, but much more to the power of love. I watched her decimation by illness and her step-by-step recovery and I know it is due to my brother, Dale, who single-handedly willed her back to health—pills, nurses and physicians notwithstanding. Thank you so much, Bub.

But it is, of course, to wee Mattie to whom my greatest thanks is owed. Both for reminding me through her own enthusiasm that shopping can be joyous—and for sitting at the dining-room table while I worked, writing her own books in tandem with mine. Let's hope this one too ends as all hers do with "happily ever after."

Sources

This project has been the flash point of my career to this point. Many of the colleagues I turned to for advice and wisdom are also great friends. Much of the understanding I share has been earned through 25 years of experience as a consultant to Fortune 100 companies. Thus, the research for this book has been more of a cumulative process, searching for illustrative anecdotes to illuminate core ideas, rather than a data-driven, quantitative analysis of marketplace phenomena. Still, there are a number of researchers to whom I referred, particularly in the search for historical perspective and context. I want to identify them here.

Introduction: I came upon Julia Christensen's work by searching the Web for insights into the "Big Box" phenomenon and stumbled upon her remarkable journey through the abandoned Big Boxes that litter the country.

Section One

Chapter 1: Hal Goldberg, a friend and colleague for more than a decade, conducted these shopping exploratories with me, specifically for this book.

Chapter 2: The stories of my grandmother's life were handed down to me by both her and my mother. The tale of floating soap I first learned in 1979, working on the centennial of Ivory soap for Procter & Gamble.

Chapter 3: The understanding of the coffee industry began for me in the mid 1980s when I worked on the Coffee Council of America's campaign, and then expanded in the late 1990s when I met Clotaire Rapaille and Brett Stover, when Brett worked for Procter & Gamble. I have also studied the Starbucks factor closely, as an ongoing phenomenon.

Chapter 4: The liquor industry, too, is one I worked in for a number of years, on a wide variety of brands.

Chapter 5: *Lovemarks* is a book written by Kevin Roberts, CEO Worldwide, Saatchi & Saatchi, published by Powerhouse Books, New York, NY.

Chapter 6: I conducted the study with clerks in behalf of a major consumer products manufacturer, attempting to develop programs with a key retailer. I am able to discuss a minor portion of it here, so long as I honor the anonymity of the client.

Section Two

Chapter 7: Three books on department stores seem seminal to me: *Counter Cultures,* by Susan Porter Benson; *Merchant Princes,* by Leon Harris; and *The Grand Emporiums,* by Robert Hendrikson.

Chapter 8: Peter Connolly was a walking encyclopedia of information about all manner of retailing, and his contribution to my understanding of specialty retailing was thrilling.

Chapter 9: Ian Rattray and Tom Magness of RattrayplusMagness were extremely kind to volunteer their expertise and free time to help me understand the grocery store muddle.

Chapter 10: My own understanding, research and consulting work with a variety of manufacturers and retailers over the years has informed my understanding of Wal*Mart and other discounters, as well as club stores.

Chapter 11: Work with Ian and in the tobacco industry, as well as packaged foods guided my initial understanding of the convenience store world, which was then augmented by work I'd done in with Jiffy Lube, while at Faith Popcorn's BrainReserve (and which was also covered in Faith's book *EVEolution*) and in the car industry.

Chapter 12: The infomercial world is one I first entered in the late 1980s, with Guthy-Renker. My view of this marketplace has been augmented by scores of meetings with QVC and HSN, as well as hypnosis research with shoppers about this way to buy. In the past several years, I've increasingly come to counsel marketers interested in Web-based marketing, as well.

Index